Habermas: A Very Short Introduction

VERY SHORT INTRODUCTIONS are for anyone wanting a stimulating and accessible way into a new subject. They are written by experts, and have been translated into more than 45 different languages.

The series began in 1995, and now covers a wide variety of topics in every discipline. The VSI library now contains over 500 volumes—a Very Short Introduction to everything from Psychology and Philosophy of Science to American History and Relativity—and continues to grow in every subject area.

Titles in the series include the following:

James Gordon Finlayson

HABERMAS

A Very Short Introduction

OXFORD
UNIVERSITY PRESS

OXFORD
UNIVERSITY PRESS

Great Clarendon Street, Oxford OX2 6DP

Oxford University Press is a department of the University of Oxford.
It furthers the University's objective of excellence in research, scholarship,
and education by publishing worldwide in

Oxford New York

Auckland Cape Town Dar es Salaam Hong Kong Karachi
Kuala Lumpur Madrid Melbourne Mexico City Nairobi
New Delhi Shanghai Taipei Toronto

With offices in

Argentina Austria Brazil Chile Czech Republic France Greece
Guatemala Hungary Italy Japan South Korea Poland Portugal
Singapore Switzerland Thailand Turkey Ukraine Vietnam

Oxford is a registered trade mark of Oxford University Press
in the UK and in certain other countries

Published in the United States
by Oxford University Press Inc., New York

British Library Cataloguing in Publication Data

Data available

Library of Congress Cataloging in Publication Data

Data available

ISBN 978-0-19-284095-0

Typeset by RefineCatch Ltd, Bungay, Suffolk

Printed and bound by
CPI Group (UK) Ltd, Croydon, CR0 4YY

Acknowledgements

I am grateful to all my colleagues in the Department of Philosophy at the University of York. I greatly appreciated discussing ideas with Marie McGinn and Stephen Everson. Tom Baldwin was all I could have wished for in a colleague and head of department, and I benefited greatly from his friendship, encouragement and encyclopaedic knowledge of philosophy. Above all Christian Piller was both a good friend, departmental neighbour, and conversation partner, whom I made find out more about Habermas than he bargained for, and whose insightful questions always left me thinking more deeply and more clearly than I had before. In 2003, I was fortunate to have the opportunity to teach Habermas's discourse ethics to an excellent class of students at the University of York. I gained ideas from the contributions of Robin Howells and Alexander Perry. I am indebted also to Matt Brown, Juliana Sokolová, Sonja Schnöring, John-David Rhodes, Charlie Burns and William Outhwaite, all of whom read and or commented on drafts of the book; to Marsha Filion, the commissioning editor at Oxford University Press, Alyson Lacewing and Peter Butcher at Refinecatch, who helped me to make order out of managed chaos. I would especially like to thank Dr. Ting-Ming Li and Connie Dibiasio both of whom, in different ways showed me care, generosity, and kindness, over the last few years. Finally, my parents Kathryn and Jon Finlayson, and Juliana deserve special mention, for their love, support and goodwill, upon which I have been able to rely in difficult times.

Contents

Preface:
Who is Jürgen Habermas?

Jürgen Habermas is one of the most important and widely read social theorists in the post-Second World War era. His theoretical writings are influential in many different areas of the humanities and social sciences. Students of sociology, philosophy, politics, legal theory, cultural studies, English, German, and European studies will all undoubtedly come across his name at some time. There are several reasons why his work has such a wide influence. To begin with, Habermas is an interdisciplinary theorist. His range of reference is prodigious. He is the very opposite of what the sociologist Max Weber (1864–1920) called a 'specialist without spirit', that is the academic who never ventures beyond the narrow domain of his own expertise. Because his work transcends the disciplinary boundaries that most academics and students work within, most of his readers have only ever encountered one facet of his work. Furthermore, Habermas has been writing for nearly fifty years and has produced a huge amount of work. In addition to his profile as a social and political theorist, he is one of the foremost public intellectuals in Europe today. He is the doyen and inspiration of the democratic left in Germany and, in keeping with the tenets of his philosophy, makes frequent critical interventions – as a citizen, rather than as an academic – in the German and European public spheres on matters of general cultural, moral, and political concern.

To keep this book short, I have provided very little information about Habermas's life. This is not because it is uninteresting, though the lives

1. Jürgen Habermas

of academics rarely make for ripping biographies, but because I believe the work is more important than the man. (That said, I shall not go so far as Martin Heidegger who, when writing about the philosopher Aristotle, noted only that 'he was born at such and such time, he worked and died'.) Habermas's work was informed and motivated by the momentous historical events he lived through, in particular by the end of the Second World War in 1945, the emergence of the Federal Republic of Germany from its economic and social ruins, the Cold War, the student protests of 1968, the fall of the Berlin Wall in 1989, and the demise of the Soviet Union.

Habermas was born in Düsseldorf in 1929. He was brought up in a middle-class German family who uncritically adapted to the Nazi regime without actively supporting it. His own political views first took shape in 1945, when he was 16. Towards the end of the war, like nearly all healthy German adolescents of his age, he joined the Hitler Youth movement. After the war, when he viewed the Holocaust film documentaries and followed the proceedings of the Nuremberg trials, his eyes opened to the horrifying reality of Auschwitz and the full extent of the collective moral catastrophe of the Nazi period.

As a young man he studied philosophy in Göttingen, Zurich, and Bonn. He was no radical. Between 1949 and 1953 he immersed himself in the work of Martin Heidegger. However, he soon became disillusioned with him, not so much because of Heidegger's membership of and public support for the Nazis, but because of his subsequent evasiveness, his refusal to express any sorrow for his actions, to acknowledge them and put them behind him. In 1949 the first government of the Federal Republic of Germany was established, led by the conservative Konrad Adenauer. The young Habermas's relation to Heidegger, which began with hopeful enthusiasm but soon turned to feelings of disappointment and betrayal, was symptomatic of his relation to the whole Adenauer regime: in his view it represented a collective and calculated refusal to acknowledge and break with the past.

2. **Martin Heidegger. As a student Habermas engaged with his work. Later he was highly critical of Heidegger's silence about his membership of the Nazi party.**

In 1954 Habermas obtained a doctorate with a dissertation on the German Idealist philosopher Friedrich Schelling. He then turned to the work of Herbert Marcuse and the early Karl Marx, and two years later became the first research assistant of the philosopher Theodor W. Adorno at the Institute for Social Research at Frankfurt. Habermas was moved by the experience of his teachers at Frankfurt, Adorno and Max Horkheimer, both of German Jewish origin, and both of whom had an understandably ambivalent sense of belonging to German tradition. From them Habermas learned how to identify with his own German traditions from a critical distance, which enabled him, as he put it, 'to continue them in a self-critical spirit with the scepticism and the clear-sightedness of the man who has already once been fooled' (AS, 46). In this period Habermas's work became more radical and more sympathetic to Marx. Too much so for the liking of Horkheimer, the Institute's director, who took exception to Habermas's openly Marxist views and engineered his departure from the Institute. In 1958

3. Konrad Adenauer, the first Chancellor of the Federal Republic of Germany

Habermas left Frankfurt for the University of Marburg, where in 1961 he received his Habilitation. Thereafter, he became Professor of Philosophy at Heidelberg and, in 1964, returned to take up the post of Professor of Philosophy and Sociology at the University of Frankfurt. During this time of political ferment, Habermas famously fell out with the student radicals, with whom he was broadly speaking sympathetic, when he provocatively termed their policy of out and out confrontation with all authority 'left-fascism'. From 1971 to 1983 he was the director of the Max Planck Institute in Starnberg. In 1983 Habermas returned to teach philosophy at the University of Frankfurt, where he established his reputation as a leading social theorist, and as a respected voice of the democratic left in West Germany.

In November 1989 the Berlin Wall fell, and in the aftermath Habermas witnessed at first hand the unification of Germany. He was among those who were highly critical of the way the unification process was conducted. In the early 1990s Habermas became increasingly interested in the work of the American political philosopher John Rawls, in his conception of liberalism, and in the tradition of American constitutional democracy. Habermas's critics on the left often paint a caricature of his career, according to which he began as a Marxist critic of capitalism and ended up as a defender of American liberal democracy. This caricature, though superficially plausible, is simplistic and based on an inability to grasp the complexity of his political and intellectual allegiances. Habermas was as much critic of Marxism as Marxist critic, and has always had grave misgivings about both capitalism and liberalism. Yet he counts West Germany's successful appropriation of the traditions of Western democracy as its greatest cultural achievement, even if he values these traditions more negatively, as a way of 'breaking with the wrong continuities' of his own political culture, than positively. For just this reason the German sociologist Ralph Dahrendorf went so far as to dub him, not without a certain irony, 'Adenauer's true grandson' (BR, 88–9). In all this complexity, and in spite of the great changes in the intellectual and political climate of the last fifty years, there is an extraordinary continuity to Habermas's intellectual and political vision.

I have sketched the psychological motivation and the biographical origins of Habermas's ambivalent relation to Germany and his enduring misgivings about nationalism. However, one should avoid the temptation to personalize these aspects of his work. It is easy to forget that the inherent complexities and tensions of recent German history and politics are alive and actual. This is made vivid to public visitors to the transparent dome of the Reichstag in Berlin, from where one can both look out, toward the Brandenburg Gate and the new Holocaust memorial, and also look right down into the parliamentary chamber below.

No social and political theory captures these complexities and tensions as nicely, and uses them to better advantage, than Habermas's. They

4. Holocaust memorial, Berlin, with the Brandenburg Gate and the new transparent dome of the Reichstag in the background

ground his cosmopolitanism, his support for the European Union, his distrust of nationalism and defence of constitutional patriotism, and his moral universalism. Habermas's philosophy is at once thoroughly German, and not the least parochial.

Retired from his post in Frankfurt since 1994, Habermas lives and writes in Starnberg and teaches part-time in the United States. He still regularly appears in print, and is as active a political and cultural commentator as he ever was. Recently he has written on subjects as diverse as bioethics, gene technology, Iraq, terrorism, cosmopolitanism, and American foreign policy after 9/11.

Most of this book is given over to discussion of Habermas's mature theory, the work that appeared between 1980 and the present. I have devoted less space to his occasional political writings. There is no implied judgement here of the relative importance of Habermas's life as a public intellectual and his career as an academic; it is just that his theory is so much harder to grasp than are his political opinions and cultural observations, which are written for a lay audience and can stand alone.

Habermas is, in a very German and nowadays somewhat unfashionable way, a purveyor of grand theory. He asks big questions about the nature of modern society, the problems facing it, and the place of language, morality, ethics, politics, and law within it. His answers are complex and wide-ranging, having been painstakingly pieced together from his knowledge of several different disciplines. Moreover, his major works are forbiddingly long and technical. He does not write for beginners, and reading his work for the first time can be a frustrating experience. While he concentrates on the big picture, he often leaves it to his collaborators and followers to fill in the details at a later date. Sometimes individual pieces of the argument are missing. At the same time, he is in constant dialogue with his critics, and frequently reformulates his ideas in response to them, making small adjustments the implications of which are not always obvious. For all these reasons, it is easy for readers who lack the big picture and do not know what is of central and what is of only marginal importance to lose their bearings. One aim of this book is to give the bigger picture, by placing the different parts of his work in the context of the whole project. To that end I shall begin by offering an outline of Habermas's entire body of mature work. It divides up into five research programmes:

1. the pragmatic theory of meaning;
2. the theory of communicative rationality;
3. the programme of social theory;
4. the programme of discourse ethics;
5. the programme of democratic and legal theory, or political theory.

Each programme is relatively self-standing, and makes a contribution to a separate area of knowledge. At the same time, however, each stands in a more or less systematic relation to all the others.

Habermas's pragmatic theory of meaning, together with his theory of communicative rationality, provide the guiding ideas of his social, ethical, and political theory. In turn, these three research programmes mutually support each other. I call them research programmes because each of them is still ongoing. Each programme answers a different set of

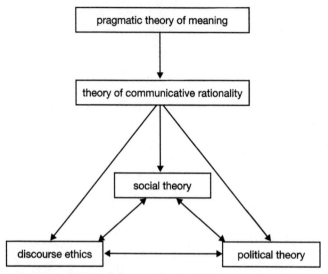

5. **Overview of Habermas's research programmes**

questions, by combining insights from different disciplines. I give a brief synopsis of each programme in the Appendix at the end of the book. In the following chapters I go through these programmes in roughly the chronological order in which Habermas conceived them.

Abbreviations

TCA 1   *The Theory of Communicative Action*, vol. 1 (Cambridge: Polity Press, 1984)

TCA 2   *The Theory of Communicative Action*, vol. 2 (Cambridge: Polity Press, 1987)

TIO   *The Inclusion of the Other*, tr. C. Cronin and P. De Greiff (Cambridge: Polity Press, 1998)

TPF   *The Past as Future: Jürgen Habermas Interviewed by Michael Haller*, tr. Max Pensky (Cambridge: Polity Press, 1994)

YAGI   'Yet Again German Identity: A Unified Nation of Angry DM-Burghers?' in *New German Critique*, 52, Winter (1991): 84–101.

List of illustrations

Chapter 1
Habermas and Frankfurt School critical theory

The Frankfurt School

Habermas is best known in the English-speaking world as the author of *The Theory of Communicative Action*, of various essays on discourse ethics, and of *Between Facts and Norms*, the works in which, roughly speaking, his social, moral, and political theory respectively are developed. Habermas is also known as the leading light of the second generation of Frankfurt School theorists, and his work is best understood as the fruit of an ongoing response to the critical theory of the first generation of Frankfurt School theorists.

The Frankfurt 'school' as it has come to be known, was a group of philosophers, sociologists, social psychologists, and cultural critics who worked in the period before and after the Second World War for the privately financed Institute for Social Research, based in Frankfurt. These thinkers, who published their work in the Institute's *Journal for Social Research*, worked loosely speaking within a common paradigm; that is, they shared the same assumptions, asked similar questions, and were all influenced by the dialectical philosophy of G. W. F. Hegel (1770–1831) and Karl Marx (1818–1883). The modern German tradition of dialectical philosophy in which they worked, sometimes called Hegelian-Marxism, was by no means the dominant one at the time. They were an intellectual minority, opposed to the reigning

European tradition of neo-Kantianism, and the Anglo-Austrian tradition of logical empiricism. This is how the retrospectively adopted talk of the 'Frankfurt School', and of Frankfurt School theory, should be understood.

6. Max Horkheimer, director of the Institute for Social Research, in Frankfurt

Max Horkheimer (1895–1973), the patrician director of the Institute, was chiefly responsible for developing the paradigm of 'critical theory' during the 1930s.

In Horkheimer's view, critical theory was to be a new interdisciplinary theoretical activity which supplemented and transformed the dialectical philosophy of Hegel and Marx with insights from the relatively new discipline of psychoanalysis, from German sociology, anthropology, and less mainstream philosophers such as Friedrich Nietzsche (1844–1900) and Arthur Schopenhauer

(1788–1860). The resultant approach had four chief characteristics: it was interdisciplinary, reflective, dialectical, and critical.

The Frankfurt School were among the first to approach questions of morality, religion, science, reason, and rationality from a variety of perspectives and disciplines simultaneously. They believed that bringing different disciplines together would yield insights that were unobtainable by working within narrow and increasingly specialized academic domains. Thus they challenged the widespread assumption of the time that the empirical approach of the natural sciences was the only valid one.

Unlike what Horkheimer called 'traditional theory', which included almost everything from mathematics and formal logic to natural science, *critical theory* was reflective, or inherently self-aware. A critical theory reflected on the social context that gave rise to it, on its own function within that society, and on the purposes and interest of its practitioners, and so forth, and such reflections were built into the theory.

Together with its interdisciplinarity, the reflectiveness of critical theory was supposed to unmask what the Frankfurt School theorists considered to be the 'positivist' illusion afflicting traditional theories (such as the natural sciences), namely that the theory is just the correct mirroring of an independent realm of facts.

That dualist picture of knowledge encouraged the belief that facts were fixed, given, and unalterable, and independent of the theory. Critical theorists rejected that picture in favour of a more Hegelian, dialectical conception of knowledge, according to which the facts and our theories are part of an ongoing dynamic historical process in which the way we view the world (theoretically or otherwise) and the way the world is reciprocally determine each other.

Finally, Horkheimer maintained that a critical theory should be *critical*. This requirement comprised several distinct claims.

Generally it meant that the task of theory was practical, not just theoretical: that is, it should aim not just to bring about correct understanding, but to create social and political conditions more conducive to human flourishing than the present ones. More specifically, it meant that the theory had two different kinds of normative aim, diagnostic and remedial. The goal of the theory was not just to determine what was *wrong* with contemporary society at present, but, by identifying progressive aspects and tendencies within it, to help transform society for the better.

When the political climate of Nazism made it impossible for its members (almost all of whom were of Jewish descent) to continue their work in Frankfurt, the Institute was temporarily relocated, first to Geneva and then to the United States, where they encountered at first hand a social phenomenon that was new to them, a consumer society in hock to a Fordist model of industrial capitalism and mass production. They were struck in particular by the way in which culture had been industrialized by big Hollywood film companies, broadcasting media, and publishing firms. These giant monopolistic corporations exerted subtle techniques of manipulation and control which had the effect of making people accept and even affirm a social system that, behind their backs, thwarted and suppressed their fundamental interests. For example, the predictable happy endings of Hollywood 'B' movies provided ersatz satisfactions for mass audiences. Instead of being critical of social conditions that prevented them finding true happiness, they vicariously experienced the fictional happiness of their screen idols. Culture unwittingly played the role of an advertisement for the way things are. Horkheimer and his younger colleague Theodor W. Adorno (1903–1969), referred to this phenomenon as the 'culture industry'.

It formed a vital part of a wider tendency of capitalist society to create and transform people's needs and desires to the extent that they actually desired the dross that was manufactured for them, and

7. Theodor Adorno, musicologist, social theorist and philosopher. Habermas's colleague and mentor at the Institute for Social Research.

they ceased to want to lead fulfilling and worthwhile lives. Analysis of these phenomena furnished insights into the ways in which the consciousness of subjects could be manipulated by advertising and other means to create what the Frankfurt School theorists thought of as a false state of reconciliation. False reconciliation was brought about by the belief that the social world was rational, conducive to human freedom and happiness, and unalterable, when in fact it was deeply irrational, an obstacle to human freedom and happiness and alterable. A century before, under rather different circumstances in Prussia, Hegel had argued that a true reconciliation had been reached, namely in those social and political conditions that rational subjects could accept and affirm, because, all things considered, they satisfied their deepest interests. The Frankfurt School, under the influence of Marx and with their experience of the twentieth century, turned Hegel's optimism upside down.

By the time Horkheimer returned to Frankfurt in 1949, both he and Adorno had become more pessimistic about the chances of realizing the practical goal of critical theory – a radical transformation of society. This pessimism was grounded theoretically in the analysis set out in their famous co-authored *Dialectic of Enlightenment* (1947, but first published in 1944 as a mimeograph entitled *Philosophical Fragments*).

Adorno's and Horkheimer's analysis of Enlightenment sets the agenda for the subsequent development of critical theory. They began from the Hegelian assumption (shared by Marx) that human beings shape or determine the world around them through their mental and physical activity – or as Marx would say, through their intellectual and manual labour. Then they added an historical thesis that by the 18th century instrumental rationality, namely the calculation of the most efficient means for achieving a given end or desire, had become the dominant form of knowledge. The historical process of enlightenment privileged natural scientific and technologically exploitable forms of knowing above all others. Adorno and Horkheimer argued that the natural sciences, which make testable generalizations and predictions about external nature, are a covert form of means/ends reasoning. Anthropologically speaking, science is just an instrument that furthers man's fundamental need to master and control his environment. Technology and industry are the extension and application of this instrument.

Adorno and Horkheimer claim that the industrialized and bureaucratized modern world is formed by a process of rationalization. The 20th-century social world is the result of the actions of human beings, whose faculty of reason has atrophied to a mere calculus of the most efficient means to a given end. The increasing mathematization and objectification of nature has led to the demise of mythical and religious world views. At the same time, the concepts by which human beings come to know their world arise from specific historical and social circumstances. Adorno and Horkheimer argue that institutional life is increasingly formed by science and technology, that is by instrumental rationality. Modern forms of sociality (institutionalized forms of instrumental rationality) give rise in their turn to instrumental concepts, representations, and ways of thinking about the world: they generate a scientific, calculating, and functional mindset. A vicious spiral ensues in which instrumental rationality becomes exclusive and total.

There is a sinister aspect to the assumption that science and rationality serve man's underlying need to manipulate and control external nature: that domination and mastery are very close cousins of rationality. Not only science and technology, but rationality itself is implicated in domination. According to Horkheimer and Adorno, even primitive forms of rationality, like magic, are incipient forms of man's domination over nature and over other human beings. For magicians cast their spells in order to bring nature under control, and their having magic powers creates social hierarchies.

Ironically, then, the very process of enlightenment which was, according to 18th-century Enlightenment thinkers such as Rousseau, Voltaire, Diderot, and Kant, supposed to liberate man from nature and to lead to human freedom and flourishing, rebounds upon him. Gradually, as industrialization and capitalism take hold in the 19th century, human beings are subjected to ever more pervasive networks of administrative discipline and control, and to an increasingly powerful and untameable economic system. Instead of liberating man from nature, the process of enlightenment imprisons man, who is himself a part of nature. Instead of economic plenty, there is misery and poverty. Instead of moral progress, there is regression to barbarism, violence, and intolerance. This is the 'dialectic of enlightenment' that informed Horkheimer's and Adorno's understanding of their social world and influenced their diagnosis of its faults.

In the eyes of the young Habermas, this unwarranted pessimism blunted the critical aim of social theory. If their diagnosis was true, if enlightenment, which was supposed to bring human beings liberty and plenty, was, from its very inception, also destined to bring them unfreedom and misery, critical social theory was caught in a bind. For social theory is itself a form of enlightenment, on Adorno's and Horkheimer's very broad understanding of that term: it is a theory that should lead both to greater understanding of the social world and to its practical amelioration. In which case, as Adorno and Horkheimer acknowledge in the Preface to *Dialectic of Enlightenment*, enlightenment is both necessary and impossible: necessary because humanity would otherwise continue hurtling towards self-destruction and unfreedom, and impossible because enlightenment can only be attained through rational human activity, and yet rationality is itself the origin of the problem. This was the *aporia* that led Horkheimer and Adorno to become ever more circumspect about the concrete political aims of critical theory. (*A-poria* is a Greek word meaning literally 'no passage' and figuratively 'perplexity'.) Adorno's faith in the capacity of any theory to guide social, political, or moral emancipation soon waned to the point that he considered almost any collective political action to be premature, arbitrary, and futile. The difference between Habermas and his teachers is that while they thought the *aporia* was real, he thought it resulted from a flaw in their analysis.

Habermas's initial response

Habermas's first major work, *Structural Transformation of the Public Sphere: An Investigation of a Category of Bourgeois Society* (1962), is a constructively critical response to Horkheimer's and Adorno's conception of critical theory. Though something of a *cause célèbre* in West Germany in the early 1960s, it was not translated into English until 1993. It attempts to resolve the problems of first-generation Frankfurt School critical theory, while remaining true to its original spirit and retaining some aspects of its diagnosis of social ills.

Structural Transformation remains true to the original paradigm in several ways. First, it is interdisciplinary, combining insights from history, sociology, literature, and philosophy. Second, it aims to locate the progressive, rational aspects of modern society and to differentiate them from the regressive, irrational ones. Third, like Horkheimer and Adorno before him, Habermas employs the method of *immanent criticism*. One can also call it internal, as opposed to external criticism. The critical theorists think this approach derives from Hegel and Marx. In some respects it is closer to the Socratic mode of argumentation, which assumes the position of the interlocutor, for the sake of argument, without actually endorsing it, in order to point out its incoherence and untruth. Whatever its origins, the critical theorists aim to criticize an object – a conception of society or a work of philosophy – on its own terms, and not on the basis of values or standards that transcend it, in order to bring its untruth to light.

Structural Transformation is an immanent criticism of the category of 'the public sphere' – a phrase that translates the German word *Öffentlichkeit*, which can mean publicity, transparency, and openness. According to Habermas, the ideals of the historical Enlightenment – liberty, solidarity, and equality – are implicit in the concept of the public sphere and provide the standard of immanent criticism. For example, 18th- and 19th-century bourgeois society can be criticized for not living up to its own ideals. Equally, West German society can be criticized for having fallen short of the inclusive, equal, and transparent society foreshadowed by those ideals. Thus *Structural Transformation* cleaves to the theoretical and practical aspirations of the original paradigm of critical theory: to understand the social world and to guide social change by illuminating potentials for social change.

However, Habermas provides a significantly different historical diagnosis of the social, political, and cultural situation to Horkheimer and Adorno. Although he does not openly criticize them until nearly two decades later, long after their deaths, Habermas thought that their account of rationalization was too one-sided and pessimistic, and that their concept of the dialectic of enlightenment lacked both empirical and historical justification and conceptual coherence. His own work attempts to rescue the original idea of critical theory by combining a more nuanced and justifiable history of the Enlightenment with a more coherent model of social theory.

The concept of the bourgeois public sphere

Structural Transformation charts the emergence of a reasoning public out of the literary public of the salons, clubs, and coffee houses of 18th-century Europe, and then depicts its gradual decline and disintegration. Habermas's narrative is quite detailed and betrays an extraordinary range of reference.

At the beginning of the 18th century, the establishment of civic rights guaranteeing the individual freedoms of association and of expression and the emergence of a free press gave rise to physical spaces such as coffee houses and salons and to literary journals, in which citizens could enter into free public discussion. They were fora in which people voluntarily came together and participated as equals in public debates. These arenas were autonomous in two senses: participation in them was voluntary, and they were relatively independent of the economic and political systems. Members of the public sphere did not just transact economically through exchange and contract in the pursuit of individual profit and self-interest. The public sphere consisted in voluntary associations of private citizens united in a common aim, to make use of their own reason in unconstrained discussion between equals. Soon, a shared culture developed that, among other things, helped the participants to discover and to express their needs and interests and to form a conception of the common good. According to Habermas, a normative notion of public opinion crystallized around the conception of the common good that was established in these fragile but sheltered arenas of public discourse.

As the authority and influence of the public spread, so gradually public opinion began to function as a check on the legitimacy of the powers of unrepresentative and closed government. By checking whether laws and policies were in the common good, the public could effectively test their legitimacy. Though the public sphere came to exercise a political and social function, however, it cannot be identified or associated with any particular political institution. It was an informal sphere of sociality located somewhere between bourgeois civil society and the state or government.

The public sphere as idea and ideology

Habermas's critical theory, as expounded in *Structural Transformation*, is a variant of immanent criticism known as the criticism of ideology, or ideology criticism. In order to understand what this is, we first have to examine the notion of ideology. Adorno defines ideology as 'socially necessary illusion' or 'socially necessary false-consciousness', and the young Habermas accepts something like the same definition. Ideologies are on this view the false ideas or beliefs about itself that society somehow systematically manages to induce people to hold. But ideologies are not ordinary false beliefs, such as my false belief that there is tea in my cup when there is coffee. Rather, ideologies are false beliefs that are very widely assumed to be true, because virtually all members of society are somehow made to believe them. Moreover, ideologies are functional false beliefs, which, not least because they are so widespread, serve to shore up certain social institutions and the relations of domination they support. This is the sense in which ideologies are *socially necessary*.

Ideology in this sense can fulfil social functions in various different ways. It may make what is in fact a social and man-made institution, and hence an institution that is in principle alterable, appear to be fixed and natural. Or it may make an institution that in fact serves the interests of a narrow class of people appear to serve the interests of everyone. If everyone, for example, believes that economic laws exist naturally and independently of human beings, then workers are more likely to accept low wages in return for their labour, rather than to see this exchange as a structural injustice in need of reform. Ideology criticism, then, is a type of immanent criticism that exposes these socially necessary illusions, and thereby, it is hoped, makes the object of criticism – here the illusion-forming social structure – more fluid and susceptible to change.

According to Habermas, the concept of the public sphere is both an idea and an ideology. The public sphere is a space where subjects participate as equals in rational discussion in pursuit of truth and the common good. As ideas, openness, inclusiveness, equality, and freedom were beyond reproach. In reality, though, they were simply ideologies or illusions. For in practice, the participation in the public sphere that existed in the coffee houses, salons, and the literary journals of 18th-century Europe was always restricted to a small group of educated men of means. Property and education were the two unspoken conditions of participation. In reality, the majority of poor and uneducated people, and almost all women, were excluded. Consequently, the idea of the public sphere remained merely Utopian, an inclusive and egalitarian vision of society worthy of pursuit, but never fully realized. The concept of the bourgeois public sphere remained ideological in the second sense too. For the notion of the common good or common interest to which the shared culture of the literary and reasoning public gave rise presented what were in fact the interests of a small group of educated men of means as the common interest of all humankind.

The critical point of Habermas's approach is to show that the idea of the bourgeois public sphere was, despite all this, more than a *mere* illusion, for it was *in principle* open: whoever had independent wealth and education was, regardless of standing, status, class, or gender, entitled to participate in public debate. No one was excluded *in principle* from participation in the public sphere, though many were *in practice*. The ideal of a universally accessible, voluntary association of private people, coming together as equals to engage in unconstrained debate in the pursuit of truth and the common good was Utopian to be sure, but it was a Utopia that was, and still is, worth pursuing. And for a brief while, in the 18th century, this Utopia not only gained intellectual currency, but began to be realized, fleetingly and partially, in social and political reality.

Decline of the public sphere

The second part of *Structural Transformation* charts the disintegration and decline of the public sphere. As newspapers and magazines gradually acquired a mass circulation, so they become absorbed into giant capitalist corporations that operated in the private interests of a few powerful individuals. Public opinion gradually lost its dual autonomy along with its critical function. Instead of fostering the formation of rational opinion and reliable beliefs, the public sphere in the 19th and 20th centuries became an arena in which public opinion could be stage-managed and manipulated. The mass-media newspapers, magazines, and bestseller novels became, along with radio and television broadcasts, consumer items, which instead of promoting freedom and human flourishing actually began to stifle it. To be sure, the state, economic, and political institutions became ever more skilled at winning public acclamation and support, and therewith the appearance of legitimacy. However, this support consisted in the private opinions of servile, uncritical, and economically dependent consumers, rather than in a healthy public opinion forged through reasoned public debate.

This rather grim view of the development of 20th-century Western capitalist society was consistent with much of Adorno's and Horkheimer's account of the way the culture industry created an increasingly homogeneous mass of docile and uncritical consumers. Habermas also adopts the Frankfurt School's rather pessimistic analysis that monopoly capitalism and welfare-state liberalism in the United States led ultimately to a diminution of human freedom, and to the hollowing out of democratic politics, and did not provide a fruitful alternative to the fragile social order of Weimar Germany that capitulated to Nazism.

For all that, Habermas is much clearer and more positive than Adorno and Horkheimer ever were about the path that should have been taken. The public sphere which in fact declined and fragmented should have deepened, broadened, and continued to exert a critical and legitimating function on the political and economic systems, pushing them into arenas of democratic control. Habermas concludes *Structural Transformation* with what is in the final analysis a hopeful speculation that such a development might still be forthcoming, on the basis of existing spheres of publicity internal to organizations such as political parties. Given the right political and social conditions, the ever-widening gap between the idea of the public sphere and social and political reality might be closed again.

Habermas's conception of critical theory

Habermas is interested in the concept of the public sphere because he sees it as the origin of the ideal of a democratic politics, and as the ground of the moral and epistemic values that nourish and maintain democracy – equality, liberty, rationality, and truth. Habermas's work always differed from that of his Frankfurt School mentors in that his deep concern for individual freedom was always wedded to an interest in the fate of democratic institutions and in the prospects for the renewal of democratic politics. Accordingly, he takes a much keener interest in the concrete institutional structure of democratic society than either Horkheimer or Adorno. In his view, critical theory had to say something about what kinds of institutions are needed to protect individuals against the attractions of political extremism, on the one hand, and the depredations of a burgeoning capitalist economy, on the other.

Adorno, like Marx before him, says little or nothing about what a good or rational society should look like, and like Michel Foucault (1926–1984) after him, is highly suspicious of institutions in general. The practical aim of Adorno's critical theory is to equip individuals with the capacities that would enable them to resist integration into the fateful homogenizing institutions of capitalist society. The most important of these is individual autonomy, understood in something like Immanuel Kant's (1724–1804) sense of *Mündigkeit* (sometimes translated as maturity) – the capacity to use one's own reason and think for oneself. For Adorno, though, *Mündigkeit* is linked to emancipation in an entirely negative way: emancipation in the current situation can only mean resistance to the established order, the capacity to say 'no', to refuse to adjust or adapt to current social reality. Habermas, by contrast, wants to identify the social and institutional conditions that foster autonomy: emancipation means the creation of truly democratic institutions capable of withstanding the corrosive effects of capitalism and the state administration.

Structural Transformation therefore gives a picture of enlightenment that is much less bleak and pessimistic than *Dialectic of Enlightenment*. In the latter, rationality itself is both the fateful cause of domination and the way to its possible undoing. Adorno's and Horkheimer's theory is self-consciously aporetic; it throws a little light on a situation from which there is no way out. Habermas's theory of the public sphere, by contrast, holds up the ideal of free rational discussion between equals as one that, though presently unfulfilled, is nonetheless worthy of pursuit.

Chapter 2
Habermas's new approach to social theory

Habermas's early work

Nearly twenty years after *Structural Transformation*, Habermas published *The Theory of Communicative Action*, the first major statement of his mature theory. The intervening two decades were by no means years of silence. Quite the contrary. In this period Habermas was extraordinarily productive, publishing several important volumes. If *Structural Transformation* marked the end of Habermas's intellectual apprenticeship, these were his years of journeying. During this intellectual journey, Habermas re-equipped and repositioned himself in respect of the tradition of Hegelian-Marxism in which he had never quite been at home. He did so by developing three related lines of thought.

Habermas's protracted critical engagement with Marx and his intellectual legacy during the 1960s and 1970s centred on the assumption that labour is the basic category of human realization and that human freedom can be meaningfully conceived as the emancipation of the forces of production and the transformation of the relations of production.

As others, including the French social theorist Simone Weil (1909–1943), had pointed out before, freedom so conceived does not amount to the emancipation of human beings and the abolition

8. Karl Marx. As a Marxist social theorist, Habermas was highly critical of Marx's social theory.

of social oppression. Human relations and human interactions must not be conflated with labour and work, because the latter are relations of a subject to an object and are merely instrumental, whereas the former are relations between subjects and are largely non-instrumental. In response, Habermas embarked on a study of the evolution of normative structures and of the development of moral consciousness as a kind of complement and corrective to Marxist thought, which was too preoccupied with the development of modes of production. This gave him a much richer conception of the social, and of human association, than Marxist theories usually allowed.

The second development was that Habermas became interested in the tradition of American pragmatism forged by William James (1842–1910), John Dewey (1859–1952), George Herbert Mead (1863–1931), and Charles Sanders Peirce (1839–1914), and the not altogether unrelated hermeneutic tradition running from Wilhelm Dilthey (1833–1911) through to Hans-Georg Gadamer (1900–2002). These traditions, American pragmatism and German hermeneutics, shared an important assumption, namely that philosophy must find its home in, and preserve its link with, everyday life. Philosophical theories and concepts have to pay their way by making a difference to the lives and the experience of real people in the actual world.

Third, alongside his critique of Marxism, and his engagement with hermeneutics and pragmatism, Habermas developed a critique of technology and science, and of scientistic and positivistic ways of thinking. Although better disposed to Vienna School logical positivism than Adorno and Horkheimer had been, Habermas remained critical of the view that all knowledge, particularly knowledge of the social world, must conform to the canons of natural science. Eventually, he developed the view that the different kinds of knowledge – theoretical, practical and critical – take shape within different frameworks, and serve different human interests. Theoretical knowledge is based on the human interest in technical control over nature; practical and moral knowledge is based on the human interest in understanding one another; while critical social theory and psychoanalysis are based respectively on the collective and individual interest in emancipation, in freedom from illusion, in autonomy (*Mündigkeit*), and the realization of the good life.

Though pregnant with characteristically Habermasian themes, this early body of work is now of largely biographical and historical interest. With *The Theory of Communicative Action* (1981), Habermas's wide-ranging influences begin to settle into a coherent programme of social theory, from which his social, moral, and political theory unfold. Much of the book is given over to discussions of the sociologists Max Weber (1864–1920), Emile Durkheim (1858–1917), Talcott Parsons (1902–1979), to the Hegelian Marxist Georgy Lukács (1885–1971), and to the critical theory of Adorno and Horkheimer. This is not a literature review.

Habermas's approach is reconstructive, not historical. He proceeds by critically appropriating competing theories and historical antecedents. In defence of this approach, he argues that the paradigms of social science (unlike those of the natural sciences) do not relate to one another as historical successors; social scientists do not drop one theory in favour of a better one, for social theories relate to one another as alternatives, competing, as it were, 'on equal footing' (TCA 1, 140). Accordingly, one criterion of a good social theory is the degree to which it can engage with its antecedents and competitors, explaining and preserving their successes, while remedying their defects. To this end, Habermas offers what he calls a 'history of theory with a systematic intent', an elaborate synthetic approach, responsible for the richness, but also for the daunting length, of his major works.

Rather than concentrate on Habermas's forays into the history of social theory, which can be rather tendentious, I will focus on the systematic intent of the work. His immediate aim in *The Theory of Communicative Action* is to solve three problems that, he thinks, stymied the thinkers in the above traditions.

Three problems of social theory

1. The problem of understanding meaning in the social sciences

The problem of understanding meaning in the social sciences is the problem of interpreting (or understanding the meaning of) human actions. The word for meaning here is the German word *Sinn*. For 20th-century ears, the term *Sinn* has two very different technical uses. It was originally used by Wilhelm Dilthey and others to denote the symbolic meaning of human actions. Here it had the sense that 'meaning' does in expressions such as 'the meaning of life'. Just to confuse things, however, the same word, *Sinn*, was used by Gottlob Frege (1848–1925) to denote the way that the object to which a word or phrase referred was given to the subject. Frege distinguished the *sense* of a term that was internal to language, its

Sinn, from its reference, or *Bedeutung*, which was in the external world. 'The morning star' has a different sense from 'the evening star', but both refer to the planet Venus. For the moment, let's put the Fregean use of *Sinn* to one side.

Dilthey argued that the human sciences, or the *Geisteswissenschaften*, such as history, philosophy, law, and literature, the disciplines concerned with the study of things human, were methodologically distinct from the natural sciences. The human sciences were ways of going about understanding the social world, whereas the natural sciences had to do with the explanation of external events or natural occurrences. Dilthey argued that natural-scientific, causal explanations were insufficient to provide understanding of the mental and spiritual life of human beings. Science explained things from the outside with the help of theories supported by empirical observation. But human actions had to be grasped also from the inside, from the standpoint of subjective experience. For example, science can give an adequate physical and biomechanical explanation of how human bodies move, but that won't tell us anything about the significance of the act of running; it won't tell us whether the person running past us is hurrying, fleeing, or exercising. To understand the meaning of the action, we have to interpret it in the light of the subjective human experience of the agent.

Weber, following Dilthey, thought one had to combine external observations of human behaviour with an understanding of the 'internal' subjective meaning of the action. The latter was to be gained by interpreting human behaviour in the light of the relevant context of human purposes, values, needs and desires. Weber held that an action was subjectively meaningful, and hence intelligible, if it could be related to a suitable context of means and ends, that is, if it could be understood as having been done for a reason. By contrast it was *meaningless*, like most animal behaviour, if it could only be explained as a response to an external stimulus. Weber linked the question of the meaningfulness of an action with the question of the reason for which it was done.

Weber's theory of action, for all its advantages over Dilthey's, has numerous defects. Weber argues that the interpreter can only understand the meaning of a person's action to the extent that she can empathetically recreate or reproduce what is going on subjectively 'inside' the mind of that person, but he does not give an adequate analysis of what this empathetic understanding is. Weber has a dualistic conception of action according to which the internal mind is separate from the external body, so that the relation between them remains intrinsically mysterious. As a consequence he cannot say what the constraints on the interpretation of an action are. This means he has no way of explaining why what counts as irrational or rational from the perspective of the agent also counts as irrational or rational from the perspective of the interpreter of the action. He therefore cannot explain why the meaning of an action remains stable over time and open to view.

A more fruitful way of approaching the whole problem is to distinguish between the subjective beliefs, desires, and attitudes of the agent and their objective 'propositional' content. Once we do that, we can understand an action by reconstructing the subjective purposes or intentions of the agent as an instance of practical reasoning.

1. Smith wants to keep warm.
2. Smith has a wood-burning stove that warms his house.
3. Smith has run out of fuel for the stove.
4. Smith knows that he can get fuel for the stove by collecting and chopping firewood.
5. Hence Smith should collect and chop firewood.

This argument shows that in the circumstances Smith has reason to collect and chop firewood. If, as interpreters, we can assume that

Smith's grasp of this reasoning has caused him to collect and chop wood, then we can, on the basis of his outward behaviour, gain an adequate understanding of the meaning of his action. The meaning of Smith's action depends on the truth of propositions 1 to 4, and on the validity of the inference to 5, which are independent both of Smith's mental states and those of his interpreter.

This now more or less standard approach to the task of interpreting actions solves the problem with the Weberian account. Although Habermas does not adopt this solution, he agrees that a theory of the meaning of action depends upon a theory of linguistic meaning, and concurs with the following points.

1. To understand the meaning of an action it is not sufficient to give an external third-person description of behaviour.
2. A correct understanding of the meaning of an action depends upon a correct grasp of the reasons for which it is done.
3. Reasons and hence actions can be correctly interpreted only with the help of background knowledge of human purposes, values, needs, desires, and attitudes.
4. The meanings of an action, and the reasons for which it is done, have a content that is in principle accessible both to the interpreter and the agent, rather than privy to the agent alone.

That said, in Habermas's eyes the standard approach is flawed, for it assumes incorrectly that human beings are pre-individuated, pre-social bearers of needs and desires. Furthermore, it assumes that each individual reasons instrumentally from their own viewpoint, so that meanings that are public and shared are made to depend on reasons that are private and individual. Finally, it replaces Dilthey's hermeneutic and Weber's psychologistic conception of *Sinn* with something more akin to the Fregean conception of *Bedeutung*. By contrast, Habermas, as we will see in the following chapter, argues that linguistic meaning cannot be reduced to the truth conditions of propositions.

2. Irrationality and the problem of ideology criticism

Social theorists since Ludwig Feuerbach (1804–1883) and Karl Marx have asked why agents are so ready to maintain and reproduce institutions that hinder or even thwart the satisfaction of their interests. Why do the poor, the marginalized, and the oppressed play along with the very institutions and laws – be they religious, economic, or political – that impoverish, marginalize, and oppress them. The answer they give is that such groups behave irrationally because they hold false beliefs about what their true interests are. Marx used the technical term 'ideologies' (which we have already come across in Chapter 1) for such false beliefs. He saw that it was not sufficient for the social philosopher simply to make the oppressed agents aware of their mistaken beliefs. Social change could not be brought about just by replacing false beliefs with true ones. It is not a matter, as Plato once wrote, of pouring sight into blind eyes. Something about the society – for Marx something about its economic organization – disposed agents to acquire these ideologies and cling to them, in spite of the best efforts of social philosophers to undeceive them. Worse still, the persistence of such ideologies helped to reproduce and maintain the very oppressive social systems that gave rise to them. The practical problem for Marxist social theorists was to identify and to alter the ideology-generating mechanisms that disposed agents to act against their true interests.

Though not without a certain intuitive appeal, this explanatory strategy was flawed. For one thing, the Marxist critic of ideology has himself to have reliable information about what the ideology-generating mechanism is, and a good explanation for why his own information is not susceptible to the kinds of ideological error he attributes so widely to others. The ideology critic has two options. Either he exempts his own theory from the suspicion that it is an ideological illusion. In that case, there must be a way to avoid being deceived, and the knowledge that a deception is occurring should be enough to prevent the false beliefs from forming. (Once we have been shown the card trick, we no longer believe it is magic.) Or he does not exempt his theory from suspicion, in which case there is no more reason to believe the ideology critic than the ideology. Horkheimer, for example, grasps the first horn of the dilemma. According to his original conception of critical theory, the interdisciplinary, reflexive, and dialectical nature of critical theory was supposed to immunize it from ideology and grant the theorist privileged insights into social reality. Adorno likewise sometimes claims that an accident of upbringing has luckily inoculated him against the effects of ideology. Still, the critical theorist is in an uncomfortable position: the deeper and more sinister the illusion-forming mechanism is supposed to be, the less credible is his claim to remain unaffected by it.

For a second thing, it is now widely accepted that the interpretation of meaning is only possible on the assumption that people are in the main rational and that their beliefs are largely true. If the interpreter is willing to countenance very widespread error and irrationality on the part of the agents whose actions she is trying to interpret, she countenances too many possible interpretations of their behaviour. (Perhaps the person running past thinks he is being pursued by an invisible bear.) Thereby the interpreter robs herself of any reliable means of establishing which interpretation is correct, and hence of understanding the meaning of the actions in question. The notion of ideological illusion cannot be stretched too widely without undermining itself. If irrationality is attributed too liberally, the social world threatens to become unintelligible. Habermas's social theory, as we will see in Chapter 4, responds to this problem by recasting the notion of ideology, and the related conception of ideology criticism, in terms of his distinction between communicative and instrumental action. For Habermas, the answer is not that lots of people are, unbeknownst to themselves, behaving irrationally: it is that they are funnelled by economic and administrative systems into certain patterns of instrumentally rational behaviour.

3. The problem of social order

Like many social theorists before him, Habermas is interested in the question of how social order is possible. This question is often presented as having been raised by Thomas Hobbes (1588–1679). Hobbes wondered how a predictable and stable social order could arise out of the actions of huge numbers of discrete individuals, very few of whom know each other personally, and of whom only a very small number are at any one time or place in a position to coordinate their actions by means of an explicit agreement. Hobbes's answer was that order is produced by the laws and authority of an all-powerful ruler, backed up by the use of force and by the credible threat of punishment.

The problems associated with the 'Hobbesian' solution to the problem of social order are familiar. From the point of view of an individual, sometimes the perceived cost of breaking laws and violating norms – punishment – will be much less than the perceived benefit of getting away with it, in which case, it will be rational to break the law rather than to obey it. Theories that purport to show that obedience to established laws somehow benefits each individual – instrumental social theories – hit against the so-called 'free-rider' problem. They cannot show why people do or should obey the laws even when it appears rational to do the opposite, and to benefit personally from the obedience of other people. Hence the problem of social order has not been adequately answered.

In the face of such objections, philosophers turned to social contract theories for answers to the problem of social order. Such theories maintained that social order rests on a network of implicit or explicit contractual relations. However, it proved equally difficult, if not impossible, to explain when and how exactly this contract was entered into by the people who are supposed to abide by its terms. Moreover, as Durkheim pointed out, not everything contractual is in the contract. Rather than explain the existence of social rules and norms, the idea of a contract presupposes that a whole raft of social norms – in particular the norms that specify that contracts be honoured – are already in place.

Durkheim himself attempted to explain social order by supposing that agents conform to norms that constitute the collective moral consciousness. They do so for both positive and negative reasons. Through socialization they come to associate certain sanctions with the violation of norms, and learn to avoid these sanctions through voluntary action. At the same time, they come to feel at home in and to identify with the collective moral consciousness of the society they inhabit. The American sociologist Talcott Parsons developed this view into the rather more sophisticated theory that the possession of a system of norms and values leads to coordination and social stability. He argued that agents acquire both a disposition to rank moral (non-instrumental, other-directed) reasons above non-moral (instrumental, self-directed) reasons, and the disposition to punish those who fail to do this. So long as most people develop both dispositions, social order can be maintained even though some agents may from time to time deviate from social norms. Should the normative mechanism of ensuring conformity fail in some cases, an instrumental safety net remains in place behind it, since people will be afraid of being punished if they don't do what morality demands.

Habermas's answer to the problem of social order consists in a novel reconfiguration of different parts of all of these theories. I will sketch the basic idea very briefly. According to Habermas, human actions are always primarily coordinated by speech or language use. Whenever agents use language to coordinate their actions, they enter into certain commitments to justify their actions (or words) on the basis of good reasons. He calls these commitments 'validity claims'. We shall examine what he means by 'validity claim' and by 'validity' in the following chapters. For now it is enough to note that these commitments have a kind of *moral* status, because they are universally applicable to agents, they are unavoidable, and they give rise to obligations towards other language users. Validity claims also have a *rational* status, because they are connected with good reasons. A validity claim is a commitment to justify one's deeds and words to others. This is not merely a linguistic and semantic phenomenon. Validity claims have a practical function, since they guide the actions of social agents. Modern societies are set up so that any agent in any situation can be asked to justify their action and is pre-committed to doing so. In this way reasons provide the invisible lines along which sequences of interaction unfold, and which guide agents away from conflict. As social agents become accustomed to having their actions guided by speech and the mutual recognition of good reasons, so relatively stable patterns of social order begin to form that do not depend directly on credible threats of punishment, on shared religious traditions, or antecedent moral values.

This is a brief sketch of the basic idea underlying Habermas's mature theory. It is the basis not just for his theory of meaning and rationality, but for his social, moral, political, and legal theory as well. This means that we will not have Habermas's answer to the problem of social order fully in view until Chapter 9. But this is not to say that Habermas's moral and political theories are merely components of his social theory and that his work is just a very long and elaborate way of answering the single question of social order. Habermas's programmes of social, moral, and political philosophy are of interest in their own right, but as you will recall from the earlier diagram (Figure 5), they are also mutually supporting. That Habermas's moral and political theory also inform his social theory reflects the fact that modern societies are highly complex, and that moral norms, state laws, and economic, administrative, and political institutions are part and parcel of the social fabric.

Chapter 3
The pragmatic meaning programme

The linguistic turn and the end of the philosophy of consciousness

Habermas claims to have embarked upon a new way of doing social philosophy, one that begins from an analysis of language use and that locates the rational basis of the coordination of action in speech. He associates this new approach with a more general shift in philosophy called the 'linguistic turn'. This phrase originally designated different attempts by various 20th-century philosophers to resolve apparently intractable epistemological and metaphysical disputes by investigating the conceptual truths inherent in our use of language. The basic strategy was to treat questions of what there is, of what can be known, and of how we can know it, as questions of what we mean, or what refers and how. Habermas applies a similar strategy to the questions of the nature of the social and the possibility of social order.

Habermas's linguistic turn is not just a turn towards language, it is a turn away from what he calls 'the paradigm of the philosophy of consciousness'. They are two sides of the same coin. The philosophy of consciousness designates a very broad philosophical paradigm that can be boiled down to a few characteristic ideas.

1. *Cartesian subjectivity*: the familiar idea that there is something called the subject (or self) that is the locus of mind conceived as an interior mental realm of ideas and perceptions.

2. This often goes together with *metaphysical dualism*, the idea that there are two different kinds of substance – thinking and extended being. This is sometimes known as *Cartesian dualism*, or *mind–body dualism*, because Descartes thought the mind and the body to be fundamentally different kinds of being.

3. *Subject–object metaphysics*: This is the more general view that the world is a totality of objects standing over and against a plurality of thinking and acting subjects. It is characteristic of this idea that subjects are not thought of as being parts of the world on which they operate. (Not all such theories are versions of metaphysical dualism. For example, Hegel transforms the subject–object paradigm from within, by conceiving the world as the product of a single self-knowing subject spirit. He therefore has a monistic subject–object metaphysics.)

4. *Foundationalism*: In the narrow sense, foundationalism refers to the epistemological doctrine of the Vienna School or 'logical' positivists, that knowledge is grounded on sense data, or on a class of primitive observational sentences. In the broad sense, foundationalism refers to the epistemological quest for certainty that characterizes much of modern philosophy from Descartes onwards.

5. *First philosophy*: This is the idea that philosophy, which does not presuppose the truths established by natural science, is required in order to provide a demonstration of the validity of scientific modes of inquiry. It is common among philosophers who are foundationalists in the broad sense, for example Descartes and Kant, both of whom hold that the chief task of philosophy is to establish criteria of correct knowledge.

There are two other ideas that Habermas associates with the philosophy of consciousness, which bear more directly on social theory.

6. *Social atomism*: the idea, common to much social and political philosophy, that individual subjects are logically, ontologically, and explanatorily prior to social, political, or ethical reality. On this view, the community consists of the sum of relations between discrete, fully constituted, pre-social, pre-political subjects. The essential point of social atomism is that while individual subjects *are not* constituted by their relations with one another or with society as a whole, society or community *is* constituted by the relations between individual subjects. This has the consequence that community is not seen as bearing any intrinsic value, and that membership within it is not viewed as intrinsically valuable. Rather, the community exists in order to serve the pre-existing interests and desires of individual subjects, and membership in the community is only ever instrumentally valuable.

7. *Society is a macrosubject*: The idea that society is a kind of macrosubject can be found in Plato, Rousseau, Schiller, Hegel, Marx and Durkheim. The idea is that society is a unitary organic whole; not just a plurality or aggregate of individuals, but a kind of collective person.

Habermas does not say that every philosopher within this paradigm accepts all of its characteristic ideas. Indeed they cannot, for it is not a consistent set. Ideas 6 and 7, for example, appear to be flatly inconsistent. The point is just that these ideas have proven to be very influential and deeply rooted in modern philosophy and that Habermas rejects them all.

Working outwards from this analysis of the linguistic turn, we can make out some general features of Habermas's philosophy. To begin with, Habermas's social theory does not picture the social world as an object (or collection of objects) standing over against a plurality of subjects with which it causally interacts. The social world is not an object or a collection of objects, and is not strictly speaking something outside us. Rather, it is a medium that we inhabit. It is 'in' us, in the way we think and feel and act, as much as we are 'in' it. This is something Habermas learned from his youthful engagement with Heidegger. A second important point is that Habermas does not see philosophy as a privileged discipline, with priority over the natural sciences. Philosophy's task is to work cooperatively alongside the natural and social sciences, whence it draws its material. Where necessary, it may act as a stand-in for what Habermas calls 'empirical theories with strong universalistic claims', that is, it can help fill gaps in natural science by offering hypotheses for empirical confirmation (MCCA, 15). Finally, Habermas's social theory gives primacy to the intersubjective dimension of social reality. Society is neither an aggregate of discrete individual subjects, nor an organic unity, in which the parts subserve the end of the whole. Not only is the social not, as he says, a 'macrosubject', it is not even unitary or uniform. As we will see in Chapter 5, it is a complex and multifarious intersubjective structure, comprising distinct overlapping spheres, within which individual agents interact.

Habermas's pragmatic theory of meaning

Viewed positively, Habermas's *linguistic* turn is also equally a *pragmatic* turn. Habermas attempts to transform social theory with the help of a particular kind of theory of meaning – a pragmatic theory of meaning. In the 1970s, Habermas, influenced by his colleague at Frankfurt University, Karl-Otto Apel, came to the view that linguistic meaning was not exhausted by propositional meaning, that meaning had a 'performative-propositional dual structure', or that propositional and pragmatic meaning went hand in hand. To appreciate the position and its bearing on Habermas's theory, let us consider each of these separately.

Propositional meaning

According to what is nowadays the standard theory of meaning, the meaning of a sentence consists in its truth conditions, and to understand the meaning of a sentence is just to know what would make it true or false. The truth-conditional theory of meaning has proven to be durable and useful. For one thing, it can explain the remarkable fact about language that from a finite vocabulary of meaningful words and phrases and the grammatical rules for their combination, an infinite number of new and more complex meaningful sentences can be formed. In turn, this explains why we can understand the meaning of sentences we have never heard before.

One difficulty with the truth-conditional model theory of meaning, though, is that it seems plausible only for a small part of language, the propositional or descriptive part. It works nicely for assertions such as 'snow is white' but not so well for expressions like 'how do you do?' It seems nonsensical to claim that to know the meaning of the expression 'how do you do?' one has to know the conditions under which the sentence 'how do you do?' is true (or false). There are many such examples where language is perfectly meaningful even though it seems odd to suggest that the meaning of sentences or parts of sentences depends on their truth conditions. For this reason, Habermas thinks truth-conditional semantics is guilty of a 'descriptive fallacy'. It makes the mistake of stretching a theory of meaning that works well for some parts of language, namely propositions, which do indeed have a descriptive or representative function, to fit all language. This is one of the reasons why Habermas prefers the pragmatic theory of meaning.

Pragmatic meaning

Habermas's theory of meaning is pragmatic because it focuses not on what language *says*, but on what language *does*; it is a theory of language *use*. He begins from a definition of language by Karl Bühler (1879–1963), a German theorist of linguistics, as a 'tool with which one person communicates something to someone about the world'. Bühler assigns three functions to language corresponding to the perspective of the first, second, and third person respectively: the 'cognitive' function of representing a state of affairs; the 'appeal' function of directing requests to addressees; and the 'expressive' function of disclosing the experiences of the speaker. Bühler's diagram makes the triadic nature of communication vivid.

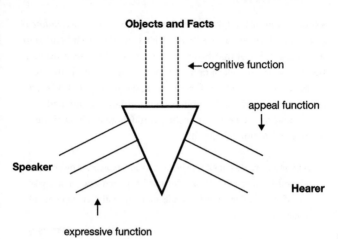

Objects and Facts

←cognitive function

appeal function

Speaker

Hearer

expressive function

9. Karl Bühler's organon model of language

He contends that any instance of language use involves a triangle comprising speaker, hearer, and world, and that the theory of language must do justice to them all. Habermas agrees. He thinks the truth-conditional theory of meaning is wrong to focus exclusively on the cognitive function and to ignore the other two, the relation between speaker and hearer. Consequently, it cannot explain adequately how we use language in a variety of different ways to communicate with one another and to coordinate our actions.

Habermas develops this view, by arguing that the pragmatic function of speech is to bring interlocutors to a shared understanding and to establish intersubjective consensus, and that this function enjoys priority over its function of denoting the way the world is. Whereas the truth-conditional theory of meaning takes propositions to be the basic meaning-bearing units of language, the pragmatic theory of meaning takes utterances to be the basic meaning-bearing units of language. An utterance consists in the words uttered by a speaker to a hearer in a certain situation for a particular reason, for example, 'the window is open'. A proposition is the content or thought the words represent, *that the window is open*. In real-life situations propositions are always embedded in utterances. It is not that Habermas rejects the truth-conditional theory of meaning out of hand. Rather, he denies firstly that it can be a general account of meaning, and secondly that it is the basic kind of meaning. He argues instead that meaning and understanding are best approached through an analysis of the pragmatic function of speech.

> One simply would not know what it is to understand the meaning of a linguistic expression if one did not know how one could make use of it in order to reach understanding with someone about something.

(OPC, 228)

Consensus and agreement

Habermas argues that the primary function of speech is to coordinate the actions of a plurality of individual agents and to provide the invisible tracks along which interactions can unfold in an orderly and conflict-free manner. Language can fulfil this function because of its inherent aim (or telos) of reaching understanding or bringing about consensus. Habermas takes it to be a fact that 'reaching understanding inhabits human speech as its telos' (TCA 1, 287). He uses the German word *Verständigung* to denote the process of reaching understanding or agreement, and the phrase *rationales Einverständnis* to denote the result of this process, the rational understanding or consensus that is reached. These words stem from the verb *sich verständigen*, which can mean to make oneself understood to someone else, but can also mean to reach an agreement with someone. This is an important ambiguity, given that the term is central to an explanation of social order. In what follows, I shall use the word 'consensus' as a convenient fudge, but we should take care not to lose sight of this ambiguity.

Habermas's theory states that the pragmatic meaning of speech consists in the way speech functions to establish a shared intersubjective consensus between interlocutors, which forms the basis of their ensuing actions. Habermas's view is that speech fulfils this function because the meaning of utterances rests on reasons. I call this the rationalist thesis because the view that meanings rest on reasons is a variety of rationalism. Habermas calls this view 'the validity basis of meaning', which in a way is more accurate, but can also be misleading because of the peculiar way in which he uses the term 'validity'. For Habermas uses the term in a pragmatic and not in a formal-logical sense. In propositional logic, the same word, 'validity', denotes a truth-preserving inferential relation between well-formed sentences. What Habermas calls validity (*Geltung* or *Gültigkeit*) is something rather different: a close relation between reasons and consensus, or as he puts it, an 'internal connection with reasons' (TCA 1, 9, 301).

The crucial point of what I am calling Habermas's rationalist thesis is that the pragmatic meaning of an utterance depends on its validity, that is on the consensus bringing reasons that can be adduced for it by the speaker. Furthermore, Habermas maintains that the meaning of actions, utterances, and propositions are essentially public or shared, and that this is because meaning depends on reasons and reasons are essentially public or shared. Shared meanings depend on shared reasons. (One can see here how Habermas's pragmatic theory of meaning reworks the theme of publicity in an entirely different idiom and at a much more abstract theoretical level than his early work.)

Now let us take a closer look at the details of the theory. Habermas argues that any sincere speech-act makes three different validity claims: a validity claim to truth; a validity claim to rightness; and a validity claim to truthfulness. These are the commitments we saw at the end of the previous chapter. Validity claims are *necessary* in the sense that they are always already understood to have been made in the act of speaking: we cannot make ourselves understood and engage in meaningful speech without presupposing and giving others to believe that we are truthful and that what we say is both right and true. As a commitment to justify, a validity claim is a commitment to supply the appropriate reasons. Habermas claims that in any act of communication the speaker must make all three validity claims. Depending on the type of speech-act, whether, for example, it is an assertion, a request, or a declaration, only one validity claim will be thematized or taken up by the hearer.

When a speaker makes a validity claim to the truth of an utterance, for example 'snow is white', she implies that there are good reasons for its being believed, and that she could, if necessary, convince the hearer of its truth on the basis of those reasons. The hearer will understand the assertion in the light of those reasons. This is a less straightforward point than it appears. The question is, when I make a validity claim to the truth of the utterance 'snow is white', am I claiming that the content of the assertion – that snow is white – is true, or that the utterance – 'snow is white' – is true? Initially, Habermas did not specify: a speaker, he claimed, 'can rationally motivate a hearer to accept his speech act offer because . . . he can assume the *warranty* for providing . . . convincing reasons that would stand up to a hearer's criticism of the validity claim' (TCA 1, 302). His present position is that truth is claimed simultaneously for the content of what is said and for the utterance.

Validity claims to rightness are, if anything, even more complicated. Habermas maintains that when I make a validity claim to the rightness of an utterance, I make a claim to the rightness of the underlying norm. For example, if I say 'stealing is wrong', I implicitly claim that I could adduce reasons that would convince my interlocutor that stealing is wrong. There are two complications here. First, Habermas thinks that moral statements such as 'stealing is wrong' are not genuine propositions and do not have truth values. To say 'stealing is wrong' is an elliptical way of saying 'do not steal', and it makes no sense to say that 'do not steal' is either true or false, since we do not predicate truth or falsity of imperatives. So the content of the moral utterance 'murder is wrong' looks like the proposition *that murder is wrong*, but that is just a roundabout way of saying that the underlying norm expressed by the imperative 'do not murder' is justified. It follows that a validity claim to rightness must be a claim to the rightness of the underlying moral norm, a commitment to provide the reasons that justify that norm.

The second complication is that 'rightness' here is ambiguous; it can mean appropriate, justified, morally permitted, or morally required. To make a validity claim to rightness could be to claim that a norm is appropriate in the given situation; it could be to claim that it is justified, it could be to claim that the actions specified by the norm are permissible, or that they are required. Habermas's view appears to be that to make a validity claim to rightness is to claim that the salient underlying norm is justified, on the basis of a special type of reason germane to the sphere of morality. When the norm is correctly applied in a given situation, it will be obvious to all concerned whether the action is being permitted, prohibited, or required.

That is enough about validity claims to rightness for the moment. I will return to them in Chapter 7. The rationalist thesis states that meaning depends on validity, because to understand the meaning of an utterance, the hearer has to be able to bring to mind (and either accept or reject) the reasons germane to its justification. The essential point here is that reason and validity, not truth, are doing the work. Instead of saying that to understand the meaning of a proposition I have to know the conditions that would make it true or false, Habermas claims that to understand the meaning of an utterance (and the same goes for actions) I have to be able to bring to mind and accept or reject the reasons that could appropriately be adduced to justify it. In Habermas's own words: 'We understand the meaning of a speech act, when we know what would make it acceptable' (TCA 1, 297).

Understanding and meaning

So far I have been presenting what Habermas calls his formal pragmatics as a theory of meaning. You have probably noticed that

37

we have been discussing questions of meaning side by side with questions of understanding. This is not surprising, given that Habermas's new approach to social theory was in part devised to solve the problem of understanding meaning. Habermas thinks that a theory of meaning should also be a theory of understanding, otherwise it abstracts the question of meaning from the context in which a speaker gives a hearer something to understand. In other words, he thinks that meaning is an intersubjective affair, rather than an objective one. (Note how his theory of meaning exemplifies his rejection of the philosophy of consciousness. On Habermas's view, meanings are not determined by the speaker's relation to the external world, but by his relation to his interlocutors; meaning is essentially intersubjective, not objective, not a bipolar relation between words and things.)

On Habermas's view, there are four different factors to understanding the meaning of an utterance:

1. the recognition of its literal meaning;
2. the assessment by the hearer of the speaker's intentions;
3. knowledge of the reasons which could be adduced to justify the utterance and its content;
4. acceptance of those reasons and hence of the appropriateness of the utterance.

Suppose I observe to my neighbour on a sunny winter's day in York: 'It is raining in Sydney.' Even though he recognizes the literal meaning of the sentence – its truth conditions – he cannot, on that basis alone, be said to have understood it, because he does not grasp the point of my uttering it. Suppose that my neighbour has informed me that he is considering emigrating to Australia. He now has a clue as to my intentions. I may be giving him a friendly warning that the grass is not always greener on the other side. Still, he might be fazed, if he thinks I have no grounds for my weather report, and may not believe it. Suppose now he discovers that I have just been on the phone to my brother in Australia. He can then bring to mind the reasons for my utterance and thus has completely understood it. In order to do this, he has to bring to mind and accept the reasons behind it, or to recognize its validity claim to truth.

Objections

More than any other programme, Habermas's theory of meaning has come in for heavy criticism. We have already raised some tricky questions. To what do validity claims to truth pertain – to the assertion or to the asserted content, or both? To what do validity claims to rightness pertain – to utterances, actions, or to the underlying norms? What concept of rightness is in play here? I cannot begin to go into all the various twists and turns that have been made in response to these criticisms. However, it would be wrong to move on from the pragmatic theory of meaning without pausing to address the two most significant objections to it.

The first one centres on the ambiguity in the meaning of Habermas's terms *Verständigung* and *Einverständnis*. The claim that social order rests on shared understandings and meanings is significantly different from the claim that social order rests on intersubjective agreement. Shared understandings and shared meanings might fall well short of agreements. Many social theorists, such as contractualists, have contended that social order rests on agreements, and that there are reasons to keep these agreements. But the claim that social order rests on shared meanings and understandings alone is something else entirely, and much more surprising if true. Habermas has often been accused of the non-sequitur that the members of a society, simply by virtue of understanding what one another mean, will adhere to the same social and moral rules.

The second objection attacks the controversial view that there are three distinct validity claims, to truth, rightness, and truthfulness. Habermas rejects the idea that there is only one kind of meaning – truth-conditional meaning – and that sentences that don't have truth conditions, such as 'How do you do?' or 'Do not steal!', are technically speaking meaningless. But his alternative, that there are three different kinds of meaning – represented by the three types of validity claim – looks even less appealing. Take the example of a mixed sentence, such as 'She slapped me in the face, which was out of order'. It looks as though the first part of the sentence makes a validity claim to truth, and the second part a validity claim to rightness. So how do we understand the meaning of the whole thing? Natural language seamlessly combines normative, epistemic, and expressive features: 'The student has plagiarized my book!' may be at once reporting a fact, expressing an attitude of disapproval because a norm has been transgressed, and disclosing subjective feelings. Habermas's theory of understanding appears to pick these various aspects apart and assign them to different validity dimensions.

Although these criticisms are well aimed, it should be remembered that Habermas's investigations into language, meaning, and truth were conceived as a preparatory study to his social theory. He was always much more interested in what the theories of meaning and understanding could do for social theory than he was in what social theory could do for them, and hence tended to cherry-pick the bits of the philosophy of language that could be made fruitful for his purposes. We should not be tempted to dismiss Habermas's entire philosophy on the grounds that there are errors or misconceptions in his theory of meaning. We should focus, rather, on the question of what insights the pragmatic theory of meaning allows him to bring to social, moral, and political theory.

Communication and discourse

The concepts of communicative action and discourse provide the central link between Habermas's pragmatic theory of meaning and his social and moral theory. The story so far is that the meaning of a speech-act depends on its validity claim. Validity claims function as a warranty or guarantee that the speaker could adduce supporting reasons that would convince the interlocutor to accept the utterance. Most of the time, the guarantee is tacitly accepted by the hearer and suffices to coordinate their interactions. This makes for a successful communicative action. When someone understands and complies with a simple verbal request, both speaker and hearer, by reaching a consensus, move seamlessly from communication to action, and actions are tacitly coordinated by validity claims.

But what happens when communication breaks down, when a validity claim is rejected by the hearer? When a hearer demands that the speaker make good her validity claim by adducing reasons for it, the agents are propelled by disagreement from an action situation into a discourse situation. Discourse is communication about communication, communication that reflects upon the disrupted consensus in the context of action. Suppose you ask me not to smoke in my office when you are present, and I demur at your request because I know that you too are a smoker. I ask you for the reasons behind your request. You may reply that you have recently given up smoking and do not wish to be tempted back into the habit. At this point, I might accept your reason and put my cigarettes away. On Habermas's view, we have entered into discourse (however briefly), reached a rationally motivated consensus (this phrase is the accepted English translation of *rationales Einverständnis*), and returned smoothly to the context of action.

There are four important points to note about discourse. First, discourse is not a synonym for language or speech, but a technical term for a reflective form of speech that aims at reaching a rationally motivated consensus (TCA 1, 42). Discourse always in principle aims at rationally motivated consensus, even if no actual consensus is forthcoming. Second, the term 'discourse' does not denote a rare and peculiar form of linguistic activity performed mainly by philosophers and pedants. It picks out the common practice of argument and justification that is woven into the fabric of everyday life. That said, discourse is not just one language game among many, for according to Habermas it occupies a privileged position in the social world. He assumes that discourse is the default mechanism for regulating everyday conflicts in modern societies. This assumption is empirical, based on observation. The function of discourse is to renew or to repair a failed consensus and to re-establish the rational basis of social order. This claim is reconstructive, based on an analysis of the practice of discourse.

Third, the concept of discourse is very closely related to the concept of a validity claim. Discourse is initiated with a challenge issued by the hearer to the speaker to make good her validity claim. As there are three types of validity claim (truth, rightness, and truthfulness), there are three corresponding types of discourse – theoretical, moral, and aesthetic.

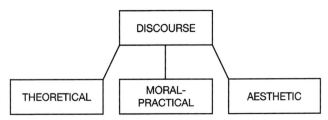

10. The three types of discourse

For example, a discourse that attempts to make good the validity claim to rightness, made by your request that I refrain from smoking, would, on Habermas's theory, be a moral-practical discourse. Any discourse arising from a challenge to a validity claim to truth is a theoretical discourse. (One has to be careful here: the term 'theoretical' is used in a much wider sense than normal.)

The fourth and final point is that discourse is a highly complex and disciplined practice, not a verbal free for all. This is because argumentation is a practice that consists in the following of certain identifiable, formalizable rules. Habermas refers to these rules as 'idealizing pragmatice presuppositions' of discourse, or rules of discourse' for short.

Rules of discourse

Habermas identifies three levels of rules. On the first level, there are the basic logical and semantic rules, such as the principle of non-contradiction and the requirement of consistency (MCCA, 86). On the second level, there are norms governing procedure, such as the principle of sincerity, namely that every participant must undertake to assert only what she genuinely believes; and the principle of accountability, that participants undertake either to justify upon request what they assert or to provide reasons for not offering a justification. At the third level are the norms that immunize the process of discourse against coercion, repression, and inequality and ensure that only the 'unforced force of the better argument' wins out. These include the rules that:

1. Every subject with the competence to speak and act is allowed to take part in the discourse.
2. a) Everyone is allowed to question any assertion whatsoever.
   b) Everyone is allowed to introduce any assertion whatsoever into the discourse.
   c) Everyone is allowed to express his attitudes, desires, and needs.
3. No speaker may be prevented, by internal or external coercion, from exercising his rights as laid down in (1) and (2) above.

(MCCA, 89)

Habermas calls the rules of discourse 'pragmatic presuppositions', because they are implicit presuppositions of the *practice* of discourse. The rules of discourse are less like the rules of scrabble or chess, which are written down somewhere, and more like the syntactic rules of a language. One can follow these rules perfectly well without being able to say what they are or knowing that one is following them. Habermas insists that these pragmatic presuppositions of discourse are *necessary*, because no one who participates in discourse – in the give and take of reasons – can avoid making them. To enter into discourse just is to incur a commitment to be sincere, to justify one's utterances, not to contradict oneself, not to exclude other participants, and so on. They are necessary in a second sense too. For agents in modern societies, there is no available alternative to communication and discourse as a way of resolving conflicts. They are too deeply engrained in the fabric of society, and in the character of individuals.

Finally, the rules of discourse are *idealizing* in that they direct participants towards the ideal of rationally motivated consensus. A discourse in which the voices of all concerned are listened to, in which no argument is arbitrarily excluded from consideration and in which only the force of the better argument prevails, will, if successful, result in a consensus on the basis of reasons acceptable to all. In real life, where time is limited and participants prone to error, discourses will only ever approximate these ideals to a greater or lesser degree. Yet they can still have a regulative effect of ensuring inclusiveness, comprehensiveness, and the absence of deception and coercion. These ideals are regulative, but they are also real insofar as the practice of argumentation in which they are inscribed is real.

The question of how one identifies rules of discourse is a difficult one. Habermas thinks that one can demonstrate that each rule is a genuine unavoidable presupposition of discourse by the device of performative self-contradiction. Sentences like, 'It is raining, but I don't believe it' or 'Snow is white, but it is not true that snow is white' are paradoxical. This is because by uttering them the speaker implicitly makes a truth claim that is explicitly denied by their content. Habermas contends that the pragmatic meaning of such sentences contradicts their propositional meaning. On similar lines, he argues that sentences such as, 'We reached a rationally motivated consensus by excluding certain people from the discourse' contains a performative self-contradiction. In this way, the device of performative self-contradiction can be used to justify rule 1, and so on for each rule of discourse. Whether a rule is a genuine rule of discourse can be ascertained by seeing whether its explicit denial generates a performative self-contradiction.

An overview of validity, truth, and rightness

Putting the various pieces together, the consensus thesis, the rationalist thesis, and the notion of discourse, brings Habermas's pragmatic conception of validity into sharper focus. The neatest and clearest way to do this is with the following validity-consensus conditional.

V→C: For any utterance 'p': if p is valid, then p is amenable to rationally motivated consensus.

This formula is my attempt to represent more formally the structure of Habermas's underlying notion of validity. A word of caution is in order. You won't find either this or the following two formulae in Habermas's writings. They are just a very concise and (I hope) helpful way to capture Habermas's rather diffuse and scattered remarks about validity, truth, and rightness, and to make their relation to one another perspicuous.

To make a meaningful utterance or to communicate is to make a validity claim, to undertake to adduce reasons that could be accepted by participants in a discourse prosecuted according to the above-mentioned rules. Not only does Habermas claim that validity, rather than truth, is the underlying concept of the theory of meaning, he maintains that truth itself can be understood as a specification of this underlying generic notion of validity. What he means is that the concept of truth has the same connection with reasons and the same pragmatic function of eliciting consensus.

T→C: For any utterance 'p': if p is true, then p is amenable to rationally motivated consensus.

Furthermore, Habermas argues that rightness can also be understood as specification of the basic underlying notion. The concept of rightness can therefore be captured with a slightly different formula.

R→C: For any norm n: if n is right, n is amenable to rationally motivated consensus.

In making a moral utterance, I tacitly endorse the underlying norm of action. Just as I commit myself, in the act of asserting 'p', to the truth of p, so when I utter the sentence, 'Theft is wrong' I endorse the underlying norm *do not steal*. The basic view is that the different validity dimensions, assertions on the one hand, moral actions and speech-acts on the other, propositions and performatives, have the same structure, and the same pragmatic function.

Habermas concludes that the concepts of truth and rightness are analogous, and the above formulae show what the analogy is supposed to be: it consists in the conditional, with validity, truth, and rightness respectively on the left-hand side and rationally motivated consensus on the right. Whatever is claimed to be valid, right, or true can necessarily gain the assent of participants in a properly prosecuted discourse. The connection is 'necessary' only in a specialized pragmatic sense, namely that speakers, hearers, and indeed agents in general cannot avoid making this connection. The 'if . . . then' connective denotes a pragmatic implication, not a logical one.

Finally, Habermas also provides us with an explanation for this analogy. Truth and rightness are analogous because they are both specifications of a single underlying norm of correctness: truth and rightness are species of the genus validity. I will say more about rightness and its relation to truth, and a lot more about the notion of discourse, later. Now we must turn to the programme of social theory proper.

Chapter 4
The programme of social theory

The basic question of Habermas's social theory is: How is social order possible? Habermas's answer is that in modern, secular societies social order rests chiefly on the basis of communicative action (action coordinated by validity claims) and discourse, which together help establish and maintain social integrity – that is, they provide the glue that keeps society together. He does this by way of a theory with two mutually supporting parts, corresponding roughly to volume 1 and volume 2 of *The Theory of Communicative Action*. The first part is mainly conceptual. Habermas makes a categorical distinction between communicative action and instrumental or strategic action, and then attempts to show that the latter is parasitic on the former. The second part is a social ontology, a theory of what society is like and what it is made of. Habermas contends that modern societies comprise two basic spheres of sociality, lifeworld and system, which are the counterparts of and homes to communicative and instrumental action, respectively.

The conceptual argument

Habermas distinguishes between communicative action, on the one hand, and instrumental and strategic action, on the other. (I am placing instrumental and strategic action in the same basket. However, there is actually an important difference between instrumental and strategic action: according to Habermas, an action is instrumental when an individual agent does something as a means to bring about a desired end; strategic action is a kind of instrumental action that involves getting other people to do things as means to realizing one's own ends. The crucial point is that both differ from communicative action.)

Instrumental action is the practical result of instrumental reasoning, the calculation of the best means to a given end. Habermas argues that there are two criteria of instrumental action: that the end of the action is determined antecedently and independently of the means of its realization, and that it is realized by a causal intervention in the objective world. Communicative action does not meet these criteria, for its inherent goal – the recognition and acceptance of a validity claim – cannot be determined independently of the vehicle of its realization, speech, and is not something that could be brought about causally.

To see why, let us return to an earlier example. In order to prevent me smoking, you could simply point the fire extinguisher at me, and say, 'If you light your cigarette I'll extinguish it with this'. Assume that I have every reason to take your threat seriously, and want to avoid being soaked. You thus succeed in getting me to comply. However, my act of compliance will not be voluntary in the normal sense of that term, because the option to refuse is not one I could seriously choose. Hence, you have caused or coerced me to comply with your request. In the alternative scenario painted in the previous chapter you attain success (my compliance with your request) on the basis of my acceptance of your reasons for it. Such acceptance or the attainment of consensus is not something you caused, but the result of a two-way process in which you have, as it were, invited me to participate.

Habermas argues not only that communicative and instrumental action are distinct types of action, but that they are basic and irreducible to other types. The distinction is both conceptual and real. There are two ways in which action can be understood and two different ways in which real agents can interact in the social world.

The second step in the argument is harder to discern. The conclusion Habermas wishes to reach is clear, but the argument for it is not. Habermas wants to show, first, that an adequate explanation of society must give pride of place to the concept of communicative action, and second, that all successful action in the real world depends on the capacity to reach consensus. To this end, he conducts an analysis of speech-act theory, in particular of the distinction between *illocutionary* and *perlocutionary* effects. This distinction was first introduced by the Oxford philosopher J. L. Austin (1911–1960), one of the originators of ordinary language philosophy. As usual, Habermas adapts the distinction for his own purposes. According to Habermas, the *illocutionary* effect of a speech-act is to elicit rationally motivated consensus, or to attain an end (for example, getting me not to smoke) by way of reaching a consensus. The earlier example nicely illustrates the point. The *illocutionary* goal of your utterance is not just to get me not to smoke, but also to get me to accept your request as valid or reasonable, *and* to voluntarily comply with it. By contrast, a *perlocutionary* effect is the effect a speech-act has apart from eliciting understanding. By warning you I might alarm you or perhaps amuse you. Perlocutionary effects are ulterior, but may be good or bad, or neither.

Habermas argues that speech-acts are self-interpreting. When I see someone running down the road in front of me, he might be fleeing or rushing or exercising. Usually, I would interpret his actions by ascribing certain propositional attitudes to him on the basis of his behaviour or outward appearance, just like we did in the case of the wood-chopper in Chapter 2. With speech-acts I have no need to do this, because their illocutionary aim is open to view. If, in a seminar, I ask a student sitting by the window to open the window, she knows what my aim is, and probably has a good idea of my motives. My speech-act manifests my intentions and aims. Now, speech can also be used strategically to attain ulterior ends or perlocutionary effects. I might try to evacuate the library by shouting 'Fire!' in a suitably alarmed and alarming manner. This attempt will only succeed if the people who hear it think I am really warning them about a fire. They can understand what I am *saying* but have no idea what I am really *doing* with the utterance, since the perlocutionary aim of my utterance is not open to view. To know the real meaning of my utterance, the hearer must somehow gain access to my latent or hidden strategic aim. But that access could only be gained by way of an illocutionary speech-act. Habermas's analysis of speech-acts is intended to show that illocutionary aims, because they are in principle open to view, are theoretically and pragmatically more basic than perlocutionary aims. He extends this point to instrumental and strategic actions in general, and infers that they are parasitic on communicative action, while the latter is basic and free-standing. On Habermas's view, your threat to turn the fire extinguisher on me may produce the required effect, but I shan't have fully comprehended your actions until I have understood and accepted the reasons for them.

Habermas's analysis is disputed, and his line of reasoning is hard to follow, but we can see the conclusion he is heading for: the meaning of speech-acts and of actions in general cannot be understood instrumentally. This is a key part of Habermas's argument against individualist and instrumental accounts of social order. Atomistic and instrumental pictures of society cannot account for the phenomenon of communication between agents, and are hence blind to its integrating effect on society. Now we can appreciate why Habermas thought that the standard answer to the question of understanding the meanings of actions combines the wrong theory of meaning with a false picture of rationality. On the standard view, the meaning of actions depends on the truth conditions of the propositional attitudes attributed to lone individuals on the basis of their external behaviour, and the logical deductions performed inside the heads of each of them. The result is a false picture of society as an aggregate of lone individual reasoners, each calculating the best way of pursuing their own ends. This picture squares with a pervasive anthropological view that human beings are essentially self-interested, a view that runs from the ancient Greeks, through early modern philosophy, and right up to the present day. Modern social theory, under the influence of Hobbes or rational choice theory, thinks of society in similar terms. In Habermas's eyes, such approaches neglect the crucial role of communication and discourse in forming social bonds between agents, and consequently have an inadequate conception of human association.

The social ontology

Habermas's social ontology is a theory of the make-up of late 20th-century society. At the heart of his theory is the distinction between lifeworld and system, two distinct spheres of social life each with its own distinctive rules, institutions, patterns of behaviour, and so on. Lifeworld and system are the respective homes of communicative and instrumental action, and here again Habermas argues that the latter – the system – depends on the former. Before we say anything about their relation, we need to examine these two terms more closely.

Lifeworld

The lifeworld is a concept for the everyday world we share with others. Edmund Husserl (1859–1938), the German philosopher who invented phenomenology and taught Martin Heidegger, first used this term in order to contrast the natural, pre-theoretical attitude of ordinary people to the world with the theoretical, objectifying, and mathematicizing perspective of natural science. Habermas does something similar. The lifeworld is his name for the informal and unmarketized domains of social life: family and household, culture, political life outside of organized parties, mass media, voluntary organizations, and so on.

These unregulated spheres of sociality provide a repository of shared meanings and understandings, and a social horizon for everyday encounters with other people. This horizon is the background against which communicative action takes place. The phenomenological metaphor of the horizon is instructive. An horizon designates the limit of a human being's field of vision under normal conditions. The field of vision is unified, but it is not a totality, since it cannot be apprehended all at once. We cannot get the whole horizon into view, because we can only see in one direction at a time. A horizon is also perspectival: the boundary shifts, albeit little by little, when we move. The boundary of a geometrical figure, by contrast, or of a piece of ground, is fixed and measurable.

By analogy, the shared meanings and understandings of the lifeworld form a unity, but not a totality. Any part of this web can be thematized or brought into view, but not all of it can be thematized at once. The contents of lifeworld are open to revision and change, but in the lifeworld change is necessarily piecemeal and gradual. Note that change, although gradual, might nonetheless be radical and thoroughgoing. In principle there is no reason why eventually every part of the lifeworld should not be revised or replaced. This is a characteristic the lifeworld shares with language, and not accidentally so, for communication is the medium of the lifeworld. Otto Neurath (1882–1945), the Vienna School philosopher of language, came up with a memorably vivid image of our linguistic situation. We are in a boat on the open sea. We cannot take the whole boat into dry dock and inspect it from outside, but we can individually replace any rotten plank of the boat and still stay afloat. The same holds for the lifeworld. On Habermas's picture, the task of carrying out running repairs to the lifeworld falls to communicative action and discourse.

The lifeworld has several functions. It provides the context for action – that is, it comprises a stock of shared assumptions and background knowledge, of shared reasons on the basis of which agents may reach consensus. So long as this shared context remains

52

in the background or, as Habermas says, unthematized, its effect will be hidden, but it will still perform its function of making the attainment of consensus likely, and indeed usual. Thus, on the one hand, it is a force for social integration. At the very same time, the platform of agreement that the lifeworld provides is the condition of the possibility of critical reflection and possible disagreement.

Overall, the lifeworld is conservative of social meaning, in that it minimizes the risk of dissent, disagreement, and misunderstanding that attends any individual instances of communication and discourse. Every time a successful communicative action takes place, a consensus is reached that feeds back into the lifeworld and replenishes it. Thus the lifeworld supports communicative action, and communicative action in turn nourishes the lifeworld by topping up the fund of shared knowledge. The lifeworld is thus able to function as a kind of bulwark against social disintegration, resisting the fragmentation of meanings and preventing the eruption of conflicts of action.

Finally, the lifeworld is the medium of the symbolic and cultural reproduction of society. It is the vehicle through which traditions are passed on, albeit through the critical lens of communication and discourse. Under normal conditions, that is in the absence of massive social upheaval, the lifeworld serves as the medium for the transmission and improvement of all kinds of knowledge: technical, practical, scientific, and moral.

System

The system refers to sedimented structures and established patterns of instrumental action. It can be divided into two different sub-systems, money and power, according to which external aims it imposes on agents. Money and power form the respective 'steering media' (that is, the inherent directing and coordinating mechanisms) of the capitalist economy, on the one hand, and the state administration and related institutions such as the civil service and state-sanctioned political parties, on the other. According to Habermas, the systems of money and power cut deep channels into the surface of social life, with the result that agents fall naturally into pre-established patterns of instrumental behaviour. For example, anyone who works for a company, whether a top executive or lowly employee, will be guided by their role into patterns of action in pursuit of financial aims. Since the aims of instrumental action are determined antecedently and independently of reaching consensus, most of the ultimate goals to which the actions of those in the system are directed are pre-set, not chosen by them. Moreover, they will not always be apparent to the agents who work to realize them. Whether they are aware of it or not, the actions of the supporters of Manchester United football club are serving the aim of making enough money for Manchester United plc to pay a dividend to their shareholders.

The chief function of the sub-systems of money and power is the material reproduction of society, that is, the production and circulation of goods and services. But they fulfil another very important function similar to that of the lifeworld, for they coordinate actions and have an integrating effect of their own. Habermas calls this effect 'system integration', in contrast to the 'social integration' provided by the lifeworld. As societies become bigger and more complex in the wake of industrialization and modernization, and as people become more mobile, the task of social integration becomes increasingly difficult. Under these conditions, systems such as the economy and the state administration ease the burden that falls to communication and discourse; they help hold society together.

We can see here already how Habermas differs from Adorno and Horkheimer, who have an almost entirely negative view of instrumental rationality in general and the capitalist economy in particular. Habermas is not hostile to instrumental rationality *per se*, nor to the institutions that embody its instrumental logic – the state and the market economy. He recognizes that they fulfil important and necessary social functions, and that abolishing them or doing without them is not an option.

Some differences between lifeworld and system

Habermas acknowledges the contributions of the system to social life, but he is keen to point out the inherent dangers with system integration. For one thing, systems of money and power steer agents towards ends that are not related to understanding or consensus. Two consequences follow. First, the full meaning or significance of our economic and administrative actions may, and often does, escape our notice. Systems institute and reinforce patterns of action in which agents conceal their aims and do not reflect on the ends of action. They thus have a kind of in-built opacity, in contrast to the lifeworld (the home of communicative action), in which the meanings of deeds and words and the ends of action tend to be open to view and intelligible. Second, the ultimate aims of agents in systems (unlike the agents in the lifeworld) are not really up to them. They can choose the means but not the ultimate ends of their actions. Consequently, one can say that the lifeworld is generally conducive to autonomy, understood as the pursuit of self-chosen ends, in a way the system is not.

This difference makes itself felt to agents in the following way. Lifeworld agents coordinate their actions through validity claims. The constraints on their actions that are generated by this process are self-imposed and internal in as much as they arise from the reciprocal recognition of validity claims. By contrast, systems of money and power impose external constraints on action that are in no way up to the agents. The system thus takes on the appearance of what Habermas calls a 'block of quasi-natural reality', an independent reality with an autonomous internal logic that escapes human control, and for which human beings cannot and need not take responsibility.

The colonization of the lifeworld

Habermas shows that modern societies consist in a fragile
equilibrium between system and lifeworld. Furthermore, because
the system is embedded in the lifeworld, and indeed parasitic on it,
the latter has priority. According to Habermas, the lifeworld is a
self-standing and self-replenishing medium, whereas the system is
not. The system can only operate on the basis of resources of
meaning that come from the lifeworld. This thesis is partly
empirical. However, Habermas also bases it on the conceptual
argument for the priority of communicative action. Since the
lifeworld embodies patterns of communicative action, and the
system embodies patterns of instrumental action, and since
communicative action is prior to instrumental action, the lifeworld
must be prior to the system.

The problem is that although the system is embedded in and
depends on the lifeworld, the former tends to encroach upon, to
displace and even destroy, the latter. This tendency of the system to
colonize the lifeworld leads to greater fragility and to disequilibrium
or instability. The notion of the colonization of the lifeworld refers
to a complex of eventually harmful historical and social processes.
To begin with, the steering media of money and power become
uncoupled from the lifeworld; the capitalist economy and the
administrative system become gradually detached from the spheres
of family and culture, and the institutions of the public sphere such
as the mass media. As the networks of instrumental action increase
in their density and complexity, so they gradually intrude into the
lifeworld and absorb its functions. Strategic decisions are left to
markets, or placed in the hands of expert administrators. The
transparency of the lifeworld is gradually obscured and the bases of
action and decision are withdrawn from public scrutiny and from
possible democratic control. As the domain of the lifeworld shrinks,
a whole gamut of what Habermas calls 'social pathologies' arise,
which include, but are not limited to, the negative effects of markets
on the non-market domains they colonize.

Pathologies resulting from the colonization of the lifeworld

1. Decrease in shared meanings and mutual understanding (anomie)
2. Erosion of social bonds (disintegration)
3. Increase in people's feelings of helplessness and lack of belonging (alienation)
4. Consequent unwillingness to take responsibility for their actions and for social phenomena (demoralization)
5. Destabilization and breakdown in social order (social instability)

Finally, since the system actually depends on the lifeworld, the whole process gives rise to instabilities and crises in the system. While Habermas is not simply anti-market, or anti-system, he is only too well aware of the potentially harmful effects that systems (such as the capitalist economy, the state, and other administrative organisations) can have on social life and on individual members of society.

Is Habermas's social theory a critical theory?

One of Habermas's chief aims in *The Theory of Communicative Action* is to provide a more fruitful, empirically sound, and methodologically coherent alternative to Adorno's and Horkheimer's critical theory. His social theory is therefore designed to be a critical theory. But in what sense? Some commentators to the left of Habermas deny that his social theory is critical at all. They see his analysis as a long-winded justification of a mixed economy and constitutional welfare state, an apology for centre-left German social democracy. This view is not just uncharitable, it is mistaken. Habermas's theory of the colonization of the lifeworld provides original, insightful, and subtle answers to the diagnostic question 'What is wrong with modern society, and why?', and illuminates the causes of the anomie, alienation, and social fragmentation that afflict modern society.

Unlike the model of ideology criticism, Habermas's social theory does not deploy the self-defeating strategy of attributing widespread error and irrationality to agents as a putative explanation for why they tolerate and perpetuate oppressive social institutions and practices. Instead, Habermas imputes to them latent or hidden strategic and instrumental aims that are inherent in the system. Oppressive social systems survive, not because individuals mistake their own interests, but because their actions fall into pre-established, bewilderingly complex patterns of instrumental reasoning. Because of the inherent opacity in social systems, the significance of actions exceeds the capacity of the agents to understand and to take responsibility for them.

Is Habermas's social theory critical in the sense that it can provide a remedy? This is perhaps the wrong question. Habermas is offering a social theory, and theories do not prescribe remedies. Of course, if the theory is correct then it would be good to protect the lifeworld from colonization by containing the systems of money and power; to ensure that there are sufficient domains of unadminstered and unmarketized social life to bring about social integration and to embed the systems of money and power. The answer, insofar as one is implied, is not to abolish markets and administration (the economy and the state), but to contain them. However, it is unclear how, if at all, even this much can be accomplished in practice, and who or what is to do it. (Interestingly, Habermas sees it less as a political than as a social task, a conclusion which is not dissimilar to *Structural Transformation* where he placed his hopes for emancipation in the reawakening of the public sphere.) In *The Theory of Communicative Action* Habermas is frank in his assessment that there is no agent, collective or individual that is up to the task. The state, insofar as it is not simply hidebound by the economy, is part of the system, and hence is one of the sources of the problem, not the answer to it. Habermas places what hopes he has of reform in a democratic welfare-state system, insofar as it can be influenced by the moral beliefs of individuals and by politically motivated, non-violent protest groups.

The trouble is that such groups – 'new social movements' as they are sometimes called – have virtually no power. And if they acquire political power, by being elected into office, they may simply be absorbed into the administrative and political system. The only agency of social reform Habermas's theory identifies is weak and unlikely to be able to halt, let alone to reverse, the process of colonization. Among all the many differences one can detect here an echo of the pessimism that haunts Horkheimer's and Adorno's social critique.

Is this a sign that Habermas's social theory is not critical enough, or simply that he is correct and realistic in his assessment that in the contemporary capitalist world not much stands in the way of the relentless expansion of markets and administration? On the first point, Habermas denies that theories can, or ever could be, critical in the Marxian sense of precipitating a revolution. Habermas has a much more modest conception of what social theory can be expected to achieve. Social theories are not themselves the vehicles of social change. They make validity claims to truth. Practically speaking, social theories are at best useful diagnostic tools that help us to differentiate between the harmful and progressive tendencies in modern society. Of course, Habermas wants to abolish social oppression, and his life and works can be understood in the light of that aim. He remains a radical and a reformer. However, he is a realist and knows that the most his social theory can directly achieve is to help us to understand the causes of social oppression.

Habermas's social theory may be thought to be uncritical in a different sense. For he deliberately refrains from making any explicitly moral criticisms of modern society. Habermas stops short of saying, for example, that the expansion of the market makes people into ruthless, calculating, self-interested individuals who think of others merely as means to their own ends. There is a good reason for this. Habermas's social theory, like the immanent criticism of Adorno and Horkheimer, is supposed to be different from moral criticism. His theory is supposed to be open about its own normative foundations, and yet not depend on a prior moral theory or conception of the good. Habermas's criticisms of modern society are in this sense functional, rather than ethical or moral. Colonization is harmful because it thwarts the good functioning of the lifeworld and deprives society of the benefits of communication and discourse – shared meanings and attitudes, social order, the feeling of belonging, social stability, and so on.

Having said that, because Habermas's notions of communication and discourse are so normatively rich, his analysis has an indelibly ethical tinge. Communicative action is based on the *mutual recognition* of validity claims. In the lifeworld, the action-coordinating mechanism of speech forces people to take other speakers, hearers, and agents and their reasons into consideration. Discourse consists in rules that ensure equal respect for and universal solidarity with all others. The ideals of equality, universality, and inclusiveness are inscribed in the communicative practices of the lifeworld, and agents, merely by virtue of communicating, conform to them. As a consequence, socialization in the lifeworld is a kind of moralization – a process of getting used to acting in accordance with these ideals. By contrast, systems inculcate the instrumental habits of treating others as the means to one's ends, and foster indifference towards the ends of others. Here, one cannot help thinking of Adorno's observation that the coldness and indifference of the middle classes was 'the principle without which Auschwitz could never have happened'. The chief difference is that in Adorno's estimation the coldness and indifference of individuals leading eventually to their cruelty towards one another was an unintended consequence of the negative side of Kantian

Habermas

moral autonomy, rational self-mastery. For Habermas, a similar phenomenon results from the de-*moralizing* effects of colonization of the lifeworld by the system, not from within morality itself. The upshot of all this is that Habermas's medical metaphor of 'social pathologies' has an unspoken and implied moral edge. On the surface, his theory is that the colonization of the lifeworld makes society malfunction; underneath, it suggests that these malfunctions produce morally flawed individuals.

Chapter 5
Habermas's theory of modernity

Habermas's philosophy has an historical as well as a systematic side. He has learned from Hegel, Marx, and hermeneutic philosophy that both the objects and the discipline of social theory have histories. As Nietzsche observed, 'only something that has no history can be defined'. Societies have histories and therefore cannot be defined, which does not mean that they cannot be explained, just that their explanation has to give consideration to these histories. Habermas's philosophy does this after a manner (albeit one that is likely to incense historians). So far, I have glossed over the fact that Habermas's social theory is a diagnosis and critique of *modern* forms of social life, and that discourse ethics is a justification and elucidation of *modern* morality. Now it is time to bring the theory of modernity and modernization into sharper focus. Doing so will help to shed light on the hidden moral dimension of Habermas's social theory. By showing how closely intertwined morality and modernity are, it will show why the harmful social effects of colonization have an impact on the morals of a community.

At some level, modernity designates a period (or a set of ideas closely associated with a period) with a beginning in time. Whether that period is now past, or still unfolding, and whether, if it is past, we should happily bid it farewell, was a much-debated question in the 1980s when *The Theory of Communicative Action* was published. (Happily, the period in which that was a pressing and important question now appears to be over.) However, modernity is more than a period. It designates the social, political, cultural, institutional, and psychological conditions that arise from certain historical processes.

Modernity in this sense is related to, but distinct from, the various aesthetic works and styles that fall under the label 'modernism'. As an artist, one has a choice whether or not to embrace 'modernism'. Modernity is not like that. You may come to modernism (or not), but modernity comes to you. Although it is reasonable to talk about Habermas's 'theory' of modernity, as I am doing here, it is not a separate programme, like discourse ethics, but a collection of ideas and assumptions that are woven into all the various programmes.

Roughly speaking, there are two halves to the theory of modernity. There is a very wide-ranging historical narrative of the development of Western society from the end of the medieval period to the late 20th century. Of special significance is the sub-plot concerning the emergence in that period of secular morality from a Christian religious tradition. In addition, Habermas offers a highly ambitious, reconstructive account of the logic of social development – a theory of social evolution. Let us look at each of these in turn.

The historical account

Modernization and the differentiation of the value spheres

We have already seen some of Habermas's views about the origins and nature of modern societies. On Habermas's account, modernization is a process comprising several related developments, some of which we have already met. First, there was a massive growth in knowledge, particularly in the natural sciences, from the 17th century onwards. Medieval science, an unreliable method of attributing supposedly explanatory properties to substances on the basis of piecemeal observations, was largely based on the authority of Aristotle. Gradually, this gave way to a more systematic approach that married precise techniques of measurement with mathematical theory formation, and a new method of formulating and testing predictive hypotheses. So successful did the new sciences turn out to be that their rise to prominence led (over several centuries and in combination with other factors) to the decline of the authority of the Aristotelian tradition, to the waning of the authority of the Church, and to their eventual replacement by the epistemic authority of natural science and reason. In its turn, Habermas contends (following Max Weber), this massive increase in technically useful knowledge led to the separating out of three distinct spheres of value.

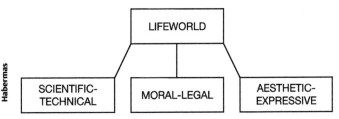

11. **The three value spheres**

It comes as no surprise that there turn out to be *three* distinct value spheres. For the differentiation of the value spheres takes place in the wake of the transfer of epistemic and practical authority from religious traditions to validity, and according to Habermas there are three distinct kinds of validity.

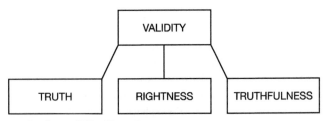

12. **The three validity dimensions**

In turn, these three dimensions of validity correlate one to one with the three spheres of discourse: theoretical, moral, and aesthetic (see Chapter 3, Figure 10). The view is that as religious world views collapse in the wake of rationalization, the problems this hands down are taken up and resolved within one of the three domains of knowledge: the natural sciences, morality/law, and the arts. Learning processes continue and knowledge deepens, but henceforth always within a single domain. The consequences are twofold. Modernity brings about a vast increase in the amount and depth of specialized knowledge, but this knowledge becomes, in the same process, detached from its moorings in everyday life, and floats free from 'the stream of tradition which naturally progresses in the hermeneutic of everyday life' (DMUP, 43). The gap between what we know, and how we live, widens.

The unfinished project of modernity

In 1980 Habermas caused a stir with his speech 'Modernity – an Unfinished Project' on the occasion of his receipt of the Adorno Prize. The speech was provocative because Habermas characteristically swam against the then strong intellectual tide of a post-modern movement anxious to bid farewell to modernity and the whole accompanying enlightenment project. Habermas's title implicitly makes two points. First, modernity is a *project* rather than an historical period; and second, this project is not yet (but can and should be) completed.

Habermas calls modernity a *project* because he sees it as a cultural movement arising in response to particular problems thrown up by the processes of modernization described above. The chief problem was to find a way to reconnect the specialized knowledge unleashed by the enlightenment process with common sense and everyday life-processes, to harness its potential for good by tying it back into the lifeworld and the common interest. This conception of modernity places what Habermas calls 'post-metaphysical' philosophy, the task of which, he contends, is to be stand-in and interpreter for the specialized sciences, at the very centre of modern life and its challenges. (It is worth recalling that Horkheimer's and Adorno's conception of critical theory addresses itself to the same discrepancy between the growth of technically exploitable knowledge, on the one hand, and the absence of any worthwhile form of social life, on the other.)

Habermas calls the modern project 'unfinished' because the problems it addresses have not yet been solved, because he thinks it futile to attempt to halt or reverse the ongoing process of modernization, and also because he thinks the proposed alternatives to modernity and modernization are worse. One such bad alternative is anti-modernity. Anti-modern thought, such as Alasdair MacIntyre's (b.1929) communitarianism, which on one reading argues for the revitalization of a Thomist tradition of moral virtues, and the later work of Martin Heidegger, which appears to welcome the return to a more rural and traditional way of life, are just different ways of dressing up a regression to pre-modern forms of living. The other bad alternative is post-modernism. Habermas suspects that the adventitious trumpeting of the end of modernity throws out the baby (the humanitarian ideals) of enlightenment along with the bathwater (the growth of instrumental rationality and the belief in the social benefits of technological and scientific development). He is allergic to all forms of relativism and contextualism, which he often conflates with irrationalism, and this may explain the in retrospect overdramatic tone of his polemic against post-modernism in *The Philosophical Discourse of Modernity*. At that time, he worried that the then influential post-modern philosophy from France might be a Trojan horse for the resurgence of irrationalism in Germany.

Habermas believes that we must not sacrifice the gains that modernity has brought with it – the increase in knowledge, the economic benefits, and the expansion of individual freedom. Completing modernity is not just accepting every development it throws at us; it means critically appropriating the cultural, technological, and economic possibilities of the modern world in the light of secular humanitarian ideals. This may be no easy task, for it requires, among other things, that 'social modernization can be encouraged in *other*, non-capitalist directions' (DMUP, 51). Completing modernity requires that the lifeworld be effectively preserved from the corroding effect of the system and, as we saw in the last chapter, there is at present no agent or force adequate to this task.

The emergence of secular morality

According to Habermas's historical analysis, modernization leads to the liberation of subjects from traditional roles and values and to their increasing reliance on communication and discourse to coordinate actions and create social order. He sums this up in what I call his modernity thesis.

> Modernity can and will no longer borrow the criteria by which it takes its orientation from the models supplied by another epoch; *it has to create its normativity out of itself*.
>
> (PDM, 7)

The talk of 'normativity' here refers to the shared meanings and understandings that arise as the result of successfully undertaken discourses. These are self-created because they are the product of communication and discourse, and in this sense are up to us as agents and participants in discourse. They are also rational, since they rest on the mutual recognition of validity claims.

One sub-plot of this general narrative is vitally important to the programme of discourse ethics. It concerns the emergence of secular morality from the monotheistic Judaeo-Christian tradition (TIO, 3–49). This tradition, Habermas thinks, contained the idea of an objectively good and just way of life in the light of which the moral question that presented itself to each individual, 'what ought I to do?', could be answered.

In the historical transition to modernity, particular and substantive questions of the good gradually separated out from formal questions of justice and moral rightness, and an ethics based on a unitary and homogeneous religious tradition was replaced by a plurality of competing conceptions of the good. Morality was gradually transformed from a repertoire of commands to a system of principles and valid norms. The valid norms of modern morality have two features: universality and unconditionality. These features, Habermas argues, are a legacy of Judaeo-Christianity. However, just because moral norms have a history does not imply that they are merely relics of a bygone era. Morality survives into modernity because it still has a point: to resolve conflicts and to help renew and maintain social order.

So far, Habermas has been recounting a history of what one might call 'really existing morality'. There is a parallel history of moral theory, which deals with the changing conceptions of morality and their theoretical expression. According to Habermas, Kant is the first moral theorist, whose theory reflects the modern conception of morality. Kant's first formulation of the categorical imperative, the 'formula of the universal law', locates the source of moral authority not in a substantive repertoire of maxims and duties, but in the formal criterion of universalization in virtue of which maxims are incorporated into the will.

> Act only on that maxim by which you can at the same time will it to be a universal law.

Since willing a maxim as a law is a free act, Kant conceives moral actions as the expression of freedom of the will. While praising Kant for wresting morality from a substantive conception of the good, and reconceiving it as a procedure for testing norms, Habermas criticizes him for assuming that each solitary individual establishes the validity of a moral norm for himself, by applying the categorical imperative to a maxim, as if it were a kind of moral mental arithmetic. In his terms, Kant conceives moral reasoning as *monological* procedure and therefore neglects its essentially social nature. In contrast, the discourse theory of morality, as Thomas McCarthy puts it, conceives morality as a collective and *dialogical* process of reaching consensus:

> The emphasis shifts from what each can will without contradiction to be a general law, to what all can will in agreement to be a universal norm.

> (MCCA, 67)

Habermas's discourse ethics is a development of a modern, Kantian conception of morality, the inner logic of which is guided by the ideals or rules of discourse.

Habermas's theory of social evolution

Habermas also has a theory of social evolution, which takes the form of a highly ambitious hypothesis that the kind of developmental learning processes that have been identified in individuals can, with appropriate modifications, be transposed to whole societies. In other words, the teleological idea that the social world is, all things considered, progressing in a certain direction, can be partially salvaged, if the analogy between individual and social learning processes can be sustained.

Lawrence Kohlberg's theory of moral development

At the fixed end of the analogy stands Lawrence Kohlberg's theory of the moral development of children. Kohlberg (1927–1987), a developmental psychologist, maintained that the moral competence of subjects develops through three invariant levels – the pre-conventional, the conventional, and the post-conventional – each of which is sub-divided into two stages. This structure of levels and stages is supposed to be 'natural' because it is culturally widespread and can in part be empirically confirmed.

Kohlberg's theory of the moral development of children

Level One: Pre-conventional morality

At Level One, the child responds to the labels of good and bad, right or wrong, but interprets these in the light of the empirical consequences of his or her actions.

Stage 1: morality is understood in terms of punishment and obedience, and the avoidance of harm to others.
Stage 2: morality is understood instrumentally as a way of satisfying one's own interests and letting others do the same.

Level Two: Conventional morality

At Level Two, meeting the expectations of one's family is valued regardless of the consequences. The characteristic attitude is one of fitting in and being loyal to the social order.

Stage 3: morality is understood as playing the role of a good boy/girl. Being good means following rules, meeting expectations, and showing concern for others.
Stage 4: morality means fulfilling one's duties, maintaining the social order, and the welfare of the society or group.

Level Three: Post-conventional morality

Level Three morality is marked by the ability to distinguish between the validity of moral norms and the authority of the groups or persons subscribing to them. Validity does not rest on the individual's identification with the group. Moral decisions reflect values or principles that are (or could be) agreed to by all individual members of a society, because they are in the common good.

Stage 5: morality is conceived as the basic rights, values, and legal contracts of a society, even when they conflict with the concrete rules and laws of a group. Subjects can distinguish between values and norms that are relative to the group, and some non-relative universal values and norms which must be protected regardless of majority opinion. Laws and duties can be based on calculations of overall utility.

Stage 6: morality is understood as whatever is in accord with the universal, self-chosen moral principles. At this stage, the reason one has for being moral is that, as a rational person, one has an insight into the validity of the underlying principles and has committed oneself to them. Validity is conferred on maxims or actions by the underlying principles. When maxims or actions conflict with principles, one acts on the principles. Examples are universal principles of justice, equality, and respect for the dignity of all human beings.

According to Kohlberg, each level, and each stage, is a phase in a learning process and superior to the previous ones in the sense that it represents a gain in complexity. Each new level preserves and improves upon the problem-solving capacities of the previous level, hence at each new level subjects manage to resolve moral problems and dilemmas more satisfactorily. Thus moral subjects, generally speaking, prefer higher levels of moral consciousness to lower levels once they have made the upward transition.

This theory is part empirical hypothesis and part moral philosophy. Some of the psychological theses, for example that agents prefer higher-level to lower-level solutions, are measurable and supported by empirical data. However, the claims about the theoretical superiority of stage 6 over stage 5 solutions (the superiority of Kantian to utilitarian morality) are supposedly established by philosophical argument. That the empirical data and the philosophical arguments support one another is then taken to be collateral evidence for the correctness of the theory.

Kohlberg's theory has come under heavy attack. Utilitarians, for example, resent being cast in the role of perpetual runners-up to Kantians, and deny that their solutions to moral problems are 'naturally' or philosophically inferior. Also, many feminists allege that there is a specifically female dimension to morality – care – the ethical significance of which Kohlberg, for various reasons, downplays or neglects. He privileges the 'rational' solutions to moral problems advanced by males, ignores the alternative solutions offered by females, and wrongly infers a thesis about child development from evidence concerning male development. Notwithstanding such controversies, Habermas endorses Kohlberg's theory of moral development with just one small difference. Just as he makes his historical account of the emergence of secular morality end not with Kant but with the discourse theory of morality, so he interpolates the discourse theory of morality at stage 6 of Kohlberg's theory (MCCA, 166–7). Cynics might raise an eyebrow here. It seems just too much of a coincidence that the historical development of modern morality, as Habermas recounts it, and developmental moral psychology, as Habermas reinterprets it, culminate in discourse theory.

Social evolution and modernization

Habermas's ambitious hypothesis is that just as the development of the moral consciousness of individuals is a learning process that can be analysed into logical stages, so is the development of society at large. After all, if the above-mentioned stages and levels are natural in individuals, this should be reflected in social structures; there should be pre-conventional, conventional, and post-conventional societies. Habermas thinks that all these levels can be identified in different historical forms of association. Societies based largely on kinship and shared religious traditions, in which morality is bound to religious and tribal authority figures, are *conventional,* whereas modern societies based on universalistic morality and on legitimate law are *post-conventional.* The social analogue of Level Two and Level Three structures of individual moral consciousness represent the kinds of rules available for collective problem-solving. If Habermas's hypothesis is correct, the process of modernization can be reconstructed as a development of increasingly complex social structures that enable individuals better to solve action problems and social conflicts.

However, there are several serious difficulties with this hypothesis. For example, it is not clear what empirical evidence could possibly confirm or disconfirm it. Another worry surrounds the alleged analogy between ontogenetic and phylogenetic development (individual and collective learning processes). It is unclear whether individual behaviour has any collective analogues. In Kohlberg's theory, it is at least clear who it is that learns – the individual child. There is a controlling consciousness, which has no analogue on the collective level. How can whole societies learn? Habermas concedes that societies learn only in the derivative sense that they provide the framework within which individuals learn to deal with conflicts and to solve problems. So it is in a very attenuated sense that the transition between conventional and post-conventional societies can be called a 'learning process'.

Habermas came up with this ambitious hypothesis in the 1970s in the course of his critical engagement with historical materialism. His theory of the development of normative social structures was supposed to complement the Marxist view that social development was determined from below by changes in the mode of production. Since then, Habermas has quietly dropped most of the theory of evolution, though he continues to deploy some of its central ideas and assumptions in his other programmes. What he has not dropped is the conviction that agents who act communicatively and who resolve conflict by means of discourse are better able to cope with the conflicts and complexities of modern social life.

Completing the modern project

Habermas's critics often complain that his work is anything but historical. He simply ransacks history for results that are congenial to his research programmes. For example, he presents moral universalism as an historical result, but he wants also to argue that it is nonetheless *an improvement* on what went before. For Habermas, the more a society is in step with the ideals of communication and discourse, that is, the more its inhabitants are oriented towards reaching consensus, the better it is for them individually and collectively. To his critics, these claims are too reminiscent of the discredited Hegelian idea that there is 'reason in history'.

There is something to these worries, but not as much as the critics suppose. Habermas denies that the guiding political and moral ideas of the modern project, even if they arise at a certain point in history, are relative to the specific cultural context that gave rise to them. He does indeed offer a qualified defence of the idea of social progress. He thinks that it can be given an empirically justified (and metaphysically respectable) interpretation: social development can be understood as a learning process, in the sense that post-conventional subjects of modern societies are better able to coordinate their actions and maintain social order than the conventional or pre-conventional subjects of pre-modern societies. That said, Habermas is anything but a dewy-eyed optimist. He rejects Hegel's teleological conception of society as an objectified form of a self-developing spirit heading towards the goal of self-knowledge. On his account, the effects of modernization on the system, the lifeworld, and their fragile equilibrium are various and its legacy ambiguous. On the negative side of the balance sheet, modernization gives rise to social pathologies – social disintegration, deracination, and feelings of alienation. On the positive side, modernity brings forth cognitive, economic, and practical gains that are worth preserving.

Habermas insists that the attempt to halt or reverse the process of modernization, as if one could flick a switch and send history into reverse, is futile. This does not mean that society is impervious to human influence. The trick is to work with the dynamic of modernity, not against it. For modernization provides resources with which the very problems it generates can be solved and the damage it inflicts contained. In the final analysis, completing the modern project means finding ways and means to ease the transition to a post-conventional society, in which subjects coordinate their actions and establish social order on the basis of universal moral principles and legitimate laws. To understand more concretely what this implies, we must turn to Habermas's moral and political theory.

Chapter 6
Discourse ethics I: the discourse theory of morality

Discourse ethics is the pivotal programme of Habermas's philosophy: *The Theory of Communicative Action* anticipates discourse ethics; *Between Facts and Norms* presupposes it. The programme is set out in two slim volumes of essays, *Moral Consciousness and Communicative Action* (1983) and *Justification and Application* (1991). There is no single major work on discourse ethics to compare with those on social and political theory. Yet discourse ethics is the normative heart of Habermas's philosophy, and develops the characteristic themes of publicity, inclusiveness, equality, solidarity, justice in the light of the pragmatic meaning programme, and the programme of social theory.

Although this is not obvious at first glance, discourse ethics is a continuation, by completely other means, of the implicit and often ignored moral dimension of Frankfurt School critical theory. In *Negative Dialectics*, Adorno writes of a 'new categorical imperative' that Hitler has imposed on mankind, namely: 'to order their thought and actions such that Auschwitz never reoccurs, and that nothing similar ever happens'. The reason the moral significance of Adorno's philosophy has, in spite of such statements, been passed over is that he denies the very possibility of living rightly in the midst of what he elsewhere calls 'a damaged existence'. After Auschwitz and Hiroshima, it is no longer possible to live a good life, or to act morally with a clear conscience. The best one can do is to resist the depredations wrought by mass culture (to resist what is sometimes called, in a dumbed-down way, 'dumbing down'), to refuse to play along with conventional morality, and to adjust to social norms. So, however striking and self-evident this moral imperative, there is an air of paradox about it.

'Learning from catastrophes' is one of the key themes of Habermas's work. Like Adorno he also lived through the Nazi period and its aftermath, and the ideal, or, more accurately, the moral bottom line expressed in Adorno's new categorical imperative, is crucial to Habermas's moral and political philosophy. The difference is that for Habermas it has concrete moral and social (and, as we will later see, political) implications: preventing the reoccurrence of Auschwitz or anything similar means preserving the lifeworld, creating conditions under which individuals are socialized into post-conventional morality, and establishing social order on the basis of demonstrably valid norms.

Moral discourse and the social function of morality

In this chapter, I focus on the discourse theory of morality and on the notion of moral discourse. The discourse theory of morality, unusually for a normative, deontological moral theory, does not directly answer the question 'What ought I to do?' Instead, it aims to uncover the conditions under which modern moral agents can successfully answer that question for themselves. Habermas's moral theory can be understood as an explication of what it means to make good a validity claim to rightness. To that extent, it is a pragmatic theory of the meaning of moral utterances. But Habermas's interest in moral semantics is subsidiary. His main aim is to see how moral theory can help answer the questions of his social theory. He is primarily concerned with questions such as: What are the underlying principles of morality?; How do we establish valid moral norms?; and What is their social function? His answer is that in modern societies valid moral norms resolve conflicts between agents and replenish the stock of shared norms.

According to Habermas, norms are behavioural rules. They usually take the grammatical form of imperatives, such as 'do not steal'. Valid (or justifiable) norms serve to coordinate our actions in the lifeworld and to stabilize our expectations of other people's behaviour. They help make the actions of others predictable, and create avenues of conflict-free action.

The hypothesis of Habermas's theory of social evolution is that modern societies are post-conventional. He takes it that, when the process of socialization goes well, mature moral agents are at Kohlberg's stage 6, the stage of a principled morality. At stage 6, agents will not be content with simply conforming to moral expectations. They might do that by consulting the Bible, by asking the advice of a wise teacher, or by copying the behaviour of their peers. Post-conventional agents know why they ought to do what they ought, and act only on principles they can justify.

On Habermas's view, a conflict arises when a validity claim to rightness is rejected. The situation thus feeds a candidate norm from the implicit background of the lifeworld into the explicit medium of discourse. One agent will feel wronged in a certain way by the actions or words of another, and will challenge the wrongdoer to explain their actions. There are many ways in which an actual dispute may be resolved. Habermas's thesis is that insofar as agents have recourse to discourse or moral discussion, its aim is to repair the consensus by establishing a norm of action that each disputant can understand and accept.

Habermas's elucidation of the moral standpoint

It is most helpful to think of Habermas's overall argument as having two halves: an elucidation and justification of the moral standpoint. The elucidation begins with the moral phenomena – our everyday moral intuitions. It is a transcendental argument. It proceeds from contingently true, empirical premises – for example, that the moral standpoint is part of the social world, that there are valid moral norms. It then investigates the conditions of their possibility. If a moral standpoint exists, there must be a principle or criterion for demarcating moral from non-moral considerations, and this principle must be implicitly contained in our moral practices. Habermas's elucidation of the moral standpoint proceeds in this manner and eventually uncovers two principles: the discourse principle (D) and the moral principle (U).

The principles of discourse ethics

Why are there two principles of discourse ethics rather than one? This is a good question, and one for which Habermas has no clear-cut answer. Eventually, he comes to the view that the discourse principle (D) is weaker and less controversial than the moral principle (U), and has already been made plausible by his theory of communication. (U) is a stronger principle which has to be established by means of an argument that makes use of (D) as a premise.

The essential point of Habermas's theory is that discourse can fulfil its social and pragmatic function all the better because it is a *dialogical* process, a process that draws people together into meaningful argument. The process of justifying a norm always involves more than one person, since it is a question of one person making the norm acceptable to another. Habermas states that (D) merely 'expresses the meaning of post-conventional requirements

---

The discourse principle (D) states that:

Only those action norms are valid to which all possibly affected persons could agree *as participants in rational discourse.*

(BFN, 107)

---

of justification'. This is jargon for the claim that (D) captures the moral agent's intuition that valid norms must command wide agreement. The label 'the discourse principle' is a little misleading, since it does not make the difference with (U) salient. (U) is just as much a principle of discourse. (D) refers to 'action norms', that is, norms in general, including legal as well as moral norms. It pertains to discourses about norms, rather than to discourse as such. Not all discourse involves norms, for example theoretical and aesthetic discourses do not. It would have probably been more accurate to call (D) the principle of the validity of norms in general.

Formally speaking, (D) has exactly the same form as the validity-to-consensus conditional (V→C) that we saw at the end of Chapter 3. It is a simple conditional, with validity on the left and consensus on the right. Note that (D) is not also a consensus-to-validity conditional (C→V), it does not say that if a norm is amenable to consensus then it is valid. Consequently (D) can only function negatively, by indicating which norms are not valid.

(D), as its official name suggests, is supposed to capture the procedure of a discourse. Assuming that a discourse has been sufficiently well prosecuted (that is, that no obvious violations of the rules of discourse have occurred), failure to reach consensus on the norm under discussion indicates that it is not valid. For example, if not everyone affected can assent to the norm 'do not eat meat', then there is no valid norm prohibiting eating meat. (D) also tells us whose agreement counts as an indication of validity. It states that if a norm is valid then all persons 'possibly affected' can accept it 'as participants in rational discourse'. This statement is not as straightforward as it appears. Consider how wide the domain of 'everyone affected' might be. If the norm is very general, the practical difficulties of allowing everyone potentially affected to take part in a discussion about it will be insurmountable. The validity of a norm will depend upon the foreseeable agreement of many people who are in practice not able to take part in the discourse. Some norms – think, for example, of the norms underlying Chinese policies of birth control permitting only one child per family – will affect people who are not yet born. People not yet born obviously cannot participate in a discourse, yet since they are 'potentially affected', the validity of a norm depends on their counterfactual assent. Because (D) requires a very wide measure of agreement, it imposes a very restrictive condition. Hence the number of cases in which discourse can actually indicate that a norm is not valid will be fairly small.

> One of Habermas's more recent formulations of (U) is that:
>
> a norm is valid *if and only if* the foreseeable consequences and side effects of its general observance for the interests and value-orientation of *each individual* could be freely and *jointly* accepted by *all* affected.
>
> (TIO, 42; translation amended)

Habermas calls principle (U) the 'moral principle', or the principle of universalizability. (U) is not itself a moral norm. It is a second-order principle, which tests the validity of first-order moral norms by checking whether or not they are universalizable. It is designed to capture the practice of moral argument and in particular the process of universalization that moral argument involves.

Moral norms are deontic rules that express obligations and have the grammatical form of imperatives like: 'Thou shalt not kill.' As we saw in the previous chapter, Habermas argues that such commands are the legacy of a Judaeo-Christian way of life. In the course of modernization, myriads of discourses have gradually sifted through the contents of that tradition, with the result that norms that still have a point (for example, 'do not steal' and 'do not kill') have been preserved, while those that do not (such as 'thou shalt not make any graven images') have been sidelined.

At first sight, principle (U) looks a little like principle (D). However, there is a major structural difference between the two principles. (U) has the logical form of a biconditional (V↔C, or V if and only if C), whereas (D) is a simple conditional (V→C, or if V, then C). (U) is therefore a much stronger principle than (D): it states that the amenability to consensus in discourse is both a necessary and sufficient condition of the validity of a moral norm. What this means in practice is that, unlike (D), (U) can function both *negatively* and *positively*. Not only does it indicate which moral norms are not valid, it can positively determine which norms are valid, and furthermore show us what moral validity or moral rightness is. A valid moral norm just is a norm that can be accepted by all affected as participants in discourse in the light of their values and interests.

The second big difference from (D) is that (U) makes validity depend on the acceptability of the 'foreseeable consequences and side effects' of the implementation of the norm. With this phrase, Habermas builds a consequentialist intuition into his deontological moral theory. He thus distances discourse ethics from Kant, who denies that the consequences of an action play any role in determining its moral worth. This is a little unusual, for deontological moral theories generally assume that the agent's intentions alone determine the moral worth of an action. (If I spit on the ground and my saliva catches a gust of wind and hits a passer by, a consequentialist theory would say that my act was morally wrong, whereas a deontological theory would say it was not, so long as my action was not reckless and had no intention to harm.)

Finally, (U) provides more information than (D) about what acceptability in discourse or rationally motivated consensus consists in. It states that all valid moral norms must give 'equal consideration' to the interests of each person concerned, and must be able to be freely accepted by all in a rational discourse (BFN, 108). In short, (U) states that a norm is valid if and only if it demonstrably embodies what Habermas calls a 'universalizable' interest.

Moral discourse as a process of universalization

To understand what a universalizable interest is, we have to look at the process of universalization by which principle (U) gets its name. Kant was the first moral philosopher to construe the moral principle as a test of universalizability. Kant's first formulation of the categorical imperative (see Chapter 5) is supposed to capture the widespread intuition that one ought not to make an exception of oneself. However, Kant's theory leads him into some well-known difficulties, because he conceives universalizability as a merely logical or rational property of maxims. For example, the maxim 'Always keep one's promises' may well be universalizable, but that itself does not explain why there is a moral obligation to keep promises. 'Early to bed and early to rise' is a universalizable maxim, but, though it might be good advice, there is obviously no such obligation. Similarly, the view that the moral wrongness of an action can be explained as a kind of logical inconsistency in the individual's reasoning is questionable. Pointing out that breaking a promise is incoherent, because it is not possible to will a world in which everyone always breaks their promises, does not show what is morally wrong with breaking a promise. We do not morally disapprove of people who are incompetent reasoners. For these reasons, Habermas conceives universalization very differently to Kant, not as an individual mental procedure but as a social one.

Habermas takes his conception of universalization from the American pragmatist social philosopher George Herbert Mead. In *Mind, Self and Society* (1934), Mead writes, 'it is as social beings, that we are moral beings'. He conceives the universalization test as a way of integrating individual human beings into the social order that he calls 'ideal role taking'. Just like players in a team game, moral agents work together by projecting themselves into the position of all other moral agents. Mead calls this adopting the attitude of the 'generalized other', but he basically means fitting in with the rest of the team.

Integrating oneself into a team turns out to be quite demanding. Integration cannot be achieved merely by thinking what the others think and doing what they do. It is a reflexive process that involves taking second-order attitudes (that is, attitudes towards one's attitudes) and modifying one's first-order attitudes in their light. The moral analogue is that each agent in society must modify what he does in the light of his expectation of what the others do, an expectation which he gains by adopting their perspective towards him and towards each other.

Mead argues that the perspective of the individual is given by his particular desires and interests: individual selves are 'constituted out of' their interests. Consequently, adopting the attitude of the generalized other means adopting a standpoint which 'takes into consideration every interest involved'. Moral behaviour is a matter of modifying one's own interests in the light of one's understanding and recognition of the interests of everyone else, a process that leads to the development of a 'larger self', which is identified with the interests of others.

Habermas draws several lessons from Mead. The first is that ideal role taking does not involve, indeed it prohibits, the switch from the first person perspective to the third-person perspective. The universalizer must not attempt to attain neutrality by breaking away from her first-person perspective as an agent in the lifeworld, and by adopting a transcendent, third-person perspective on her own situation. Moral obligations address us in the first person and it is in the first person that they should be conceived. Participants in moral discourse are not ideal reasoners or merely rational choosers. They are real people, agents in the lifeworld, allowing themselves to be guided by the rules of discourse, which makes them envisage themselves as part of what Habermas calls 'an idealized we-perspective'.

Each of us must be able to put themselves into the position of all those who would be affected by the performance of a problematic action or the adoption of a questionable norm.

(JA, 49)

The second important lesson is that an actual discourse must be carried out if this ideal extension of the finite individual perspective to what Habermas calls the regulative ideal of an 'unlimited communication community' is to come into play (JA, 51). Even if a discourse has to be extended to include non-existent people, a real discourse must actually be carried out if a norm is to be justified (MCCA, 94). The third lesson is that discourses are inherently *dialogical*. Unlike Kant's *monological* test of the universalizability of maxims, moral discourses cannot be carried out by individuals reasoning alone. Fourth and finally Habermas concludes that discourse is a process by which individuals integrate themselves into society. A properly socialized moral agent brings his individual interests and his identity into line with the collective interest. By acting on valid norms, individual agents serve the common good. Habermas takes the thesis that valid norms contain 'universalizable interests' to be equivalent with the claim that valid norms are 'equally good for all'. In this way, a kind of impartiality is achieved, but not at the cost of the abandoning the first- and second-person perspective.

The overall picture is that moral discourses require participants to put themselves in the place of all others potentially affected by a candidate norm, in order to see whether or not it can be welcomed from their perspective too. For example, wealthy people or educated people in possession of a marketable skill may be inclined to accept the abolition of social welfare on the grounds that they impose unfair tax burdens on people like them. But would they welcome the policy if they were poor and unskilled? By requiring them to exchange perspectives with the poor and unskilled, (U) eliminates norms that militate in favour of certain particular persons or groups.

The justification of (U)

Habermas's elucidation of the moral standpoint takes the form
of an analysis of the everyday intuitions of modern moral agents,
that unearths the principles of discourse ethics, (D) and (U).
These principles capture the procedure of discourse by
which agents in the lifeworld tell which moral norms are
valid, information that allows them to judge the wrongness
or permissibility of particular actions in particular
situations.

The elucidation of the moral standpoint is not a philosophical
justification of it, since it begins from moral premises. It assumes
that the moral standpoint exists and asks how this is possible.
Habermas's justification of the moral standpoint does not make
that assumption. The justification of the moral standpoint takes the
shape of a formal derivation of principle (U), the moral principle.
Habermas thinks that unless (U) can be derived formally, from
non-moral premises, the suspicion will remain that (U) is just an
'ethnocentric prejudice', that is merely an expression of a culturally
and historically contingent set of values. Unfortunately, Habermas
does not himself provide a formal derivation of the moral principle,
although he has always (perhaps too confidently) assumed that
there is one.

He does, though, tell us what the two premises are from which
(U) is to be formally derived: the rules of discourse and 'the
conception of normative justification in general as expressed
in (D)' (TIO, 43). The problem is that there is just no way to see
how (U) can be inferred logically from those premises alone.
Nothing in the rules of discourse (see Chapter 3) and the
conditional principle (D) allow Habermas to infer (U), the
biconditional (V$\leftrightarrow$C). Recall that (D) is only a simple conditional
(V$\rightarrow$C). Nothing in the rules of discourse allows Habermas to
conclude that if a norm is amenable to consensus, it must
be valid (C$\rightarrow$V). The justificatory argument, if it is to work,
needs supplementary premises.

Realistically, there is only one place Habermas can look for these additional premises – the theory of modernity. The trouble is it is highly unlikely that the modernization theory can be confirmed independently of the programme of discourse ethics. If anything, the relation of justification will go the other way. The most that can be hoped for is that the discourse theory of morality, if justified, will count as evidence for Habermas's theory of modernity. It looks, then, that in the absence of any formal derivation of (U), discourse ethics stands and falls with the plausibility of Habermas's elucidation of the moral standpoint.

Objections to Principle (U)

Let us now look at some well-known objections to the discourse theory of morality.

The redundancy objection

We have just seen how demanding the test of universalization is. According to (U), norms are valid if and only if they demonstrably satisfy a general interest of all concerned and are adopted by everyone on that basis. Since the scope of consensus aimed at by (U) and (D) is so wide (agreement of 'all concerned'), and the process of ideal role-taking is so demanding, (U) must be very restrictive. Not many candidate norms will survive such a severe test of its validity, and those that do will be extremely general.

Habermas's initial response to this objection was to deny that there would be very few valid moral norms, if his account were true. Later he concedes the point, but rather than see it as a flaw in his theory, he portrays it as a strength. Discourse ethics accurately reflects the reality of modern morality. He argues that, while it is true that the number of valid moral norms diminishes in modern multicultural societies, the ones that remain are all the more central and important (JA, 91). Habermas adduces the example of universal human rights to show that valid moral norms are indeed central and of the utmost import, and that some have found universal acceptance.

Is this a convincing response to the redundancy objection? Yes and no. It is empirically true that, if there are any universally acceptable moral norms, there are not many. So a moral theory cannot be faulted for showing this. That said, Habermas's discourse theory sets out to explain the essential social and pragmatic function of morality. Habermas's concession that there are so few valid norms makes it puzzling why moral discourse is still the default mechanism for resolving conflicts in the lifeworld and a primary means of social integration. The fewer valid norms there are, the fewer conflicts will be resolvable by moral discourse. In which case, it is hard to see why moral discourse should still be so central to the explanation of social order. The real work of holding society together is being done elsewhere, by something other than valid moral norms. There must therefore be some other reason for the persistence of moral discourse than its pragmatic success in resolving conflicts.

Besides, it is not obvious that the fact that human rights discourse is widespread and entrenched is evidence that moral discourse must be holding the social world together. The reason that people the world over are quick to assert their human rights may be that rights secure a benefit to the right-holder. Rights put others under obligations. Yet people are rarely so eager to assert and to fulfil their universal duties towards others. This gives grounds to suspect that there may be, to use Habermas's terms, systemic and ideological reasons for the growth of human rights discourse. Human rights discourse might itself be an example of the colonization of the lifeworld, rather than a source of resistance to it.

Objection to the dialogical–monological distinction

Another set of objections concern Habermas's strict distinction between dialogical and monological moral theories. We have already touched upon one of them. Habermas thinks that a monological conception of morality like that of Kant suffers by comparison with a dialogical one, because individuals reasoning alone will be more prone to errors and biases of perspective. But the number of actual participants in a moral discourse may be very small, while the domain of those affected by the norm's being generally followed may be huge. Habermas has no real grounds on which to conclude that a dialogical approach to the problem (a discourse) will be in practice epistemically superior to (more likely to be correct than) an individual monological judgement. It could be argued that so long as a norm is based on a correct assessment of the relevant reasons (for example, what everyone's interests are, and what norm satisfies those interests), it is justified. If a very small number of actual participants in discourse can establish satisfactorily that a norm is valid, then, in principle, why cannot each individual on her own? The existence of a consensus may not confer validity, as Habermas thinks, so much as indicate that each person individually has judged correctly.

The circularity objection

Finally, discourse ethics has been charged with circularity. This charge has been levelled at Habermas's derivation of principle (U), at the overall argument of discourse ethics, and at the rules of discourse. The circularity objection arises because the programme of discourse ethics assumes that morality must be justified on non-moral premises; it must be an argument that can convince even a moral sceptic, provided she is rational. On the one hand, as we have seen, the non-moral premises Habermas has to hand are not strong enough to vindicate principle (U). On the other, whenever Habermas helps himself to a richer premise – the theory of modernity or the rules of discourse – they turn out to smuggle in moral assumptions and raise the threat of circularity. The rules of discourse are a case in point. These include rule 2. c), that everyone is allowed to express his attitudes, desires, and needs. Clearly 2. c) is not a rule of discourse in general, since it grants everyone permission to express their attitudes, desires, and needs. It thus appears to have *prima facie* moral significance, and cannot count as a non-moral or non-controversial premise in an argument for (U).

However, it is by no means obvious that Habermas needs to justify the moral principle on the basis of non-moral premises anyway. Of course he must avoid vicious circularity; that is, he must not smuggle his conclusion into the premises of his argument. That does not mean that all his premises have to be morally neutral. It does mean, though, that discourse ethics won't be in a position to convince the moral sceptic, but that may be too much to ask for any moral theory.

Chapter 7
Discourse ethics II: ethical discourse and the political turn

Habermas's division of practical reason

In his original programme of discourse ethics of the 1980s, Habermas used the terms 'morality' and 'ethics' interchangeably. Only later, in 1991, did he begin to make the distinction between them. However, he kept the label 'discourse ethics' to denote the revised programme, because it was simpler than rechristening it the 'discourse theory of morality'. In fact, in the revised programme of the 1990s Habermas draws a triple distinction between moral, ethical, and pragmatic discourse, each of which designates a different use of practical reason. The real significance of the revision lies in the introduction of a separate category of ethical discourse alongside that of moral discourse, and in the way these two spheres of discourse are reconfigured in the programme of political theory.

Before we examine the nature and function of ethical discourse as distinct from moral discourse, we must turn briefly to Habermas's use of the term 'pragmatic' in pragmatic discourse. So far the term 'pragmatic' has denoted the social function or use of something. Habermas's conception of morality is *pragmatic* because it construes moral discourse as a social mechanism of conflict resolution. His theory of meaning is pragmatic, since it views language use as a way of coordinating actions and instituting social order. Here, though, Habermas introduces the term in a narrower sense. Pragmatic discourses concern the rational choice of the means to a given end. They say nothing about the choice of ends. Pragmatic discourse is the dialogical form of instrumental reasoning, and is especially germane to the political and legal domains, since politics and law are essentially concerned with what is feasible.

What is ethical discourse?

Up until the time of Hegel, ethics and morality were usually taken to be equivalent. However, the two terms represent different traditions of thinking about human life. The term 'ethics', as Habermas often notes, has both an ancient and a modern use. It stems from the ancient Greek word *ethos*, which referred both to the customs of a *polis*, or city-state, and to the habits and character of its people or citizens. In modern times, Hegel uses the term *Sittlichkeit* (commonly translated as 'ethical life') to denote the concrete way of life of a community, replete with its values, ideals, and self-understandings, on the one hand, and practices, institutions, and laws, on the other.

Habermas's conception of ethical discourse has several distinguishing features.

1. Ethical discourse is 'teleological' in the senses that it concerns 'the choice of ends' and the 'rational assessment of goals' (JA, 4). Where pragmatic discourse takes one's desired ends as given, and deliberates the best means to achieve them, ethical discourse evaluates those ends.
2. Ethical discourse evaluates ends by assessing what is 'good for me' or 'for us' (DEA, 41; JA, 5, 8). These are particular, not universal, goods. (Morality, by contrast, deals with questions of right and wrong, which insofar as they are good (or bad) are supposed to be universally good (or bad), since they affect everyone in the same way.) The notion of the good that ethical discourse puts in play relates both to the individual life history of the person and to the

collective life of the community. Habermas calls discourses concerning an individual life 'ethical-existential', and those concerning the collective or group 'ethical-political'.

3. Ethical discourse is prudential: it concerns the ways in which we organize the satisfaction of our desires and ends with a view not just to present but also to future happiness and to our happiness all things considered.

4. Ethical discourse makes salient the values that are germane to an individual's life history and to the particular tradition or cultural group to which that individual belongs. Habermas has a very specific concept of a value. A value is a basic symbolic constituent of culture or ethical life. To say that values are basic means that they cannot be analysed into anything more simple, and explained in a more primitive vocabulary, say, of preferences, desires, needs, or reasons. Values determine preferences, not vice versa. They help shape our needs, desires, and interests, which, Habermas argues, are not given to us fully formed by our biology or social heritage, but always stand in need of interpretation. Because values are tightly bound to the fabric of a particular community, each individual in the course of her socialization into the institutions and practices of that community will absorb and internalize its basic values. Hence these values will come to form a core component of the individual's self-identity. Values are thus not 'out there' like natural facts, existing independently of us. They are engrained in us and we are in the midst of them. Consequently, although individual values are susceptible to interpretation and to gradual change, they are not something from which human beings can very easily detach or abstract themselves. Finally, values are by their nature gradual, whilst norms are absolute: values admit of higher and lower degrees, whereas norms are either valid or not. While it makes little sense to say that one action is more morally wrong than another, it makes perfect sense to say that one choice is better than another.

5. Habermas's understanding of the concepts of good and of value bear upon a logical feature of ethical discourse. The advice, judgements, and orders of preference in which ethical discourses

issue, have only 'relative' or 'conditional' validity. (By contrast, the norms in which successful moral discourses issue are universally and unconditionally valid. Whereas a valid moral norm is meant to hold across different and competing cultural traditions, values only hold within a particular tradition or cultural group.)

6. Ethical discourse concerns the self-understanding of the individual or group. Whether about an individual or group, ethical questions are broadly speaking hermeneutic questions. They aim at self-clarification, self-discovery, and to an extent also self-constitution. When successful, they issue in judgements or advice about which ends, values, or interests to pursue for the sake of one's overall good (JA, 9; BFN, 151–68; DEA, 38–50).

Synopsis of the difference between ethical and moral discourse

	Ethics	Morality
Basic concept	good/bad	right/wrong just/unjust
Basic unit	values	norms
Basic question	What is good for me or for us?	What is just? What ought I to do, and why? What is right?
Validity	relative and conditional	absolute and unconditional
Type of theory	prudential, teleological	deontological
Aims	advice; judgement preference ranking	establishing valid norms; discovering duties

7. Ethical discourse makes a validity claim to authenticity (DEA, 41). It is not very clear how this validity claim fits in with the other three validity dimensions of truth, rightness, and truthfulness. Authenticity appears to be an analogue of truthfulness in the practical domain. It does not fit in with Habermas's neat triadic schema because, by the time he introduces this revision to discourse ethics, he is not so concerned to make it backwards compatible with his pragmatic theory of meaning. This lack of fit indicates that our moral conceptions are much messier than Habermas's neat conceptual distinctions make them look.

The validity and scope of ethical discourse

One of the defining characteristics of ethical discourses is that the advice in which it issues has only 'relative' or 'conditional' validity. Habermas does not say too much about what relative validity is, but we can presume that it is a question of scope. Valid moral norms are supposed to be universally binding on all participants in discourse or all concerned by its implementation, whereas ethical values or judgements are only binding upon members of the relevant group. Nonetheless, the very fact that the members of a group can collectively and freely assent to a judgement about some aspect of their conception of the good, a judgement that expresses a value they hold in common, is supposed to have some justificatory force, though, as we shall see below, not enough to outweigh any countervailing moral considerations.

Cultural groups, then, provide frameworks to which ethical values and goods relate. This raises the question of what counts as a cultural group and thus as a legitimate framework of evaluation. I think Habermas assumes this is a largely empirical sociological question. Yet it is also a matter of philosophical interest. For example, it seems obvious that talk of particular cultural groups does not cover the set of all left-handed people, all women, or all supporters of Arsenal football club. Arguably, they are all members of a totality or a set, but that membership is not of any ethical-political significance (though it may, of course, be of great ethical-existential significance to an individual person's life).

Membership of a cultural group in the relevant sense is a different kind of relation entirely. To begin with, groups have a common character that pervades many aspects of life and shapes the individuals who grow up within it, and who are socialized into it. This means that cultural groups must be large enough to maintain and reproduce themselves and their common character. Group membership is also a matter of mutual recognition, so that one counts as a member of a group only if, among other things, one is recognized as being a member of the group. Third, membership is important to the self-identification and self-understanding of individual members, and one of the primary ways by which they are identified and understood by others. Finally, membership is largely a matter of belonging. Cultural groups are not clubs, entry into which is gained by an administrative mechanism. Belonging to a group is not a simple affair. It may be the result of a long and difficult process in which the individual absorbs the group culture and is gradually accepted into it.

Such criteria show why, whatever the similarity of their experiences, all Arsenal fans, all left-handed people, and all women, are not cultural groups in the sense required by Habermas's notion of ethical-political discourse. This is important since he must not allow that every set of people who share an interest, however large or small, constitutes a cultural group that can serve as the framework of ethical evaluation. In England fox hunters and lovers of field sports like to present themselves as belonging to a cultural group of country dwellers that is misunderstood by the urban majority. On these grounds they protest against the government's proposal to ban fox hunting. However, their self-conception is confused and misleading. Of course, everyone who has an interest in fox hunting can freely agree that fox hunting is good, just as anyone who has an interest in playing Bridge or listening to Bob Dylan can agree that these are good. Such agreement does not mean that fox hunting is justified ethically or otherwise. These interest groups or lobby groups are not groups in the relevant sense. They are a collection of individuals with shared preferences. They do not form the kind of traditions that are in need of clarification by ethical discourse. The very question of what the genuine interests of the group are is already answered by its mere existence. Compare English fox hunters for a moment with the Bushmen (and women) of the Kalahari, who value hunting as part of their common way of life. For such a people, a prohibition on hunting would genuinely threaten their way of life and their cultural identity.

The social function of ethical discourse

The social function of ethical discourse differs according as it concerns the life history of an individual or the culture of a group. Given that modern societies comprise competing traditions and cultural groups with different and discrepant conceptions of the good, shared values may be more likely to be the source of group conflicts in modern multicultural societies than they are the key to their resolution. To take a random example, in Britain conflicts frequently arise concerning arranged marriages of the second and third generation daughters of immigrant parents. For their part, the immigrant parents want to pass on their customs and practices, in the light of which their wishes and expectations for their daughters are formed. Often, however, the daughters have formed their preference and expectations in the light of values like individual autonomy and romantic love that they have assimilated from the culture in which they have grown up.

On Habermas's theory, given that values may be the source of intractable dispute, one response is to try to resolve that dispute by avoiding any appeal to values. That is just what moral discourse according to (U) purports to do. Norms are not values. They are behavioural rules, anchored in the communicative structure of the lifeworld, based on very general and universally shared interests. Hence, moral discourse is the first recourse for disputing parties in the lifeworld. However, given the scarcity of universally valid norms, such conflicts may not be open to moral regulation, in which case, ethical discourse could help. In such a situation, ethical discourse will involve in the first instance a discussion and clarification of the all things considered best interests of the person concerned. It will also inevitably involve a critical appropriation of the values endemic to her culture, and reflection on her personal situation and individual life history.

Like moral discourses, ethical discourses cannot be conducted by anyone else except the persons uniquely concerned. No one, least of all moral philosophers, can determine their results in advance. Yet we can imagine two plausible scenarios. In one scenario, the parents, while noting their daughter's wish to choose her own husband, override it and decide the matter in what they consider to be her and their best interests and marry her off against her wishes. Her options then are active defiance of her parents' wishes or reluctant compliance. An alternative scenario is that those concerned mutually adjust, refine and reinterpret their interests and values, in order to avoid conflict. The parents might, for example, allow that a marriage be arranged in consultation with the bride, so that she does do not feel that her individual autonomy and possibility of romantic love is being sacrificed on the altar of cultural tradition alien to her generation. Such a scenario is possible because cultures are internally complex, multifaceted, and people's particular interests are open to revision and interpretation in the light of different aspects of it.

This alternative points to an important feature of ethical discourse. Recall Habermas's thesis that modernization involves the critical appropriation of traditions. Traditions are altered, gradually, by being reflected upon in ethical discourse. Some strands are self-consciously continued, others lapse. Values, conceptions of the good, and self-understandings are not fixed. They are always in the process of being reinterpreted. Collective identities (as well as individual ones) must be thought of as a kind of project, in the literal sense: we are suspended between what we find ourselves as, and what we want ourselves to be.

The priority of the moral over the ethical

Habermas observes that in the course of modernization questions of universal rightness (justice) gradually separate out from questions of the good life, and a plurality of discrepant and competing concrete conceptions of the good slowly emerges from a by and large homogeneous religious tradition. On these grounds, he regards it as a mistake to see ethics and morality as two competing approaches to the same questions. Ethics and morality are distinct but complementary components of our everyday self-understanding. Habermas takes it to be a phenomenological asset that discourse ethics can make room for both moral and ethical discourse, instead of opting for one or the other.

Habermas and the priority of moral discourse

The notion of ethical discourse comes to play an increasingly important role in Habermas's thought as he becomes more interested in democratic and legal theory. Nevertheless, he continues to insist on the priority of the moral. He argues for its priority on several grounds. First, pragmatically speaking, moral discourse is the default mechanism for the resolution of conflicts between agents in the lifeworld, because, unlike ethical discourse, it cuts values out of the justification process, thereby circumventing a source of intractable conflict. Second, moral discourse has a certain social-ontological priority over ethical discourse in virtue of the fact that (U), and by extension each valid norm, is anchored in the communicative structure of the lifeworld. Normative rightness is not a cultural value, not even a very widespread one. It embodies the communicative ideals of equal respect for all and universal solidarity contained in the rules of discourse. It is a specification of validity, analogous to truth, without which communicative agents in modern societies could not live as they do. Finally, Kohlberg's model of moral development and modernization theory support the thesis of the priority of morality. Post-conventional subjects have abstract self-identities that are not rooted in any particular tradition. This manifests itself in a disposition to embrace discursive procedures for deciding moral issues reflectively, before asking substantive questions about who one is and what would be the best life.

The upshot is that morality sets limits to ethics. According to Habermas, ethical discourses are sources of justification that already operate within the bounds of moral permissibility. Suppose ethical reflection yields a judgment which violates a moral norm. To return to our example, suppose the parents conclude the best course of action is to force their daughter to return to their country of origin against her will. In that case, the participants would be propelled into a moral discourse concerning the rightness of the action, and may also have to contend with breaking the law. In Habermas's scheme, however well justified an ethical consideration, however important a particular cultural value might be, it can always be overridden by a valid moral norm. Moral norms, when available, trump any ethical values that conflict with them.

Rawls and the priority of the right

On this point discourse ethics bears comparison with later work of the American political philosopher John Rawls (1921–2002), who defends the thesis of the priority of the right over the good. The similarity of views is no accident since the revisions to discourse ethics in the 1990s are very much influenced by Rawls. Rawls thinks that the right and the good are complementary concepts. The right here must be understood in relation to Rawls's thesis that a practicable modern conception of justice as fairness must be 'political not metaphysical'. Rawls observes that modern societies are no longer culturally homogeneous; they comprise a plurality of world views and 'comprehensive doctrines' competing for loyalty. In view of this fact, the legal and constitutional framework of a well-ordered society must not depend on, or presuppose, the truth of any one particular world view. This is the negative meaning of the thesis that justice must be political not metaphysical. Hence Rawls recommends a 'method of avoidance' whereby dispute is minimized because controversial moral and religious values are cut out of the process of political justification.

Positively viewed, political justifications appeal to general ideas and values that command widespread assent across all different cultures and world views. They are part of what Rawls calls a contingently 'overlapping consensus' of values. One must be careful here. When Rawls uses the term 'consensus', he does not mean the process of reaching understanding or agreement and the result of that process. For Rawls, a belief or idea is part of an overlapping consensus when it is the case that everyone, regardless of tradition or world view, has reason to accept it. It does not matter on what grounds they accept it. One of the most crucial of these is the very idea of society as a fair system of cooperation between free and equal citizens. This, Rawls argues, is a moral idea, but is not bound to any one comprehensive doctrine: it finds resonance in all of them.

Rawls contends any conception of the right (or justice) that meets this political criterion of justification is reasonable or justified, though not in virtue of its being true or probably true. The question of its truth/untruth is not germane to its political justification. What is germane is that it provokes the least controversy and commands the most loyalty. In this way, the right (or justice) sets out a liberal political framework within which each individual is free to revise, refine and pursue her conception of the good to the extent that this is compatible with everyone else's freedom to do likewise. The right is thus dependent on the existence of various competing conceptions of the good (or comprehensive doctrines) which can gain support from citizens. The right and the good are complementary: 'justice draws the limit, the good shows the point'.

Habermas versus Rawls

Clearly, there is a large measure of agreement between Habermas and Rawls. Both accept the fact of reasonable pluralism. Both agree that there is a fundamental distinction between something like morality/the right and ethics/the good and that an adequate theory has to make room for both. Furthermore, they agree that the right enjoys priority over the good. Finally, they agree that there is a functional or pragmatic aspect to the priority of the right. The impartiality of the concept of the right ensures that it commands widespread acceptance across cultures and world views, and thus facilitates social stability and harmony.

However as the famous debate between the two philosophers shows, there are areas of disagreement too. Habermas assumes that in a culturally pluralist society profane and secular moral considerations take precedence, whereas Rawls is more agnostic on this point. Whether morality is profane or religious is a matter of metaphysical controversy. Habermas objects that Rawls's *political* conception of justice sacrifices its cognitive status (its rational acceptability) to its functional or instrumental aim of ensuring social stability. Principles of justice are justified as reasonable simply because they happen to be accepted by all, regardless of whether they deserve to be. By contrast (U) guarantees that all and only those norms are justified that are rationally acceptable (that is, that deserve to be accepted by all) on the grounds that they demonstrably embody a universalizable interest. According to discourse ethics moral rightness is internally linked to validity and is analogous with truth. Habermas thus takes himself to have provided 'epistemic' and 'cognitive' grounds, not just functional ones, for the priority of the moral: he has shown that morality is knowledge, rather than the expression of contingently held values.

For his part, Rawls rejoins that Habermas, by basing discourse ethics on his controversial theory of meaning (and by insisting that morality be secular) is advancing just one more metaphysical doctrine. Rawls's method of avoidance extends also to philosophical and metaethical theories (that is theories about what morality is) not just to world views and metaphysical doctrines. Political philosophy, he argues, should avoid taking needless theoretical hostages to fortune. In one respect, Rawls is clearly right.

Habermas's programme of discourse ethics is closely tied to a whole bundle of controversial philosophical views, about meaning, communication, and so forth. That said, Habermas's chief concern is to deny that the discourse theory of morality is metaphysical in the specific sense that it expresses particular cultural values. Moral discourse captures a formal and universal procedure, to which there is no viable alternative, and by means of which participants determine for themselves, in concert, what is morally right. Thereby it establishes the bounds of moral permissibility within which ethical discourse can go to work. (This argument is somewhat weakened by his failure to provide a formal derivation of principle (U).)

The comparison between Rawls and Habermas on the priority question is instructive, but also a little misleading when abstracted from the context of their respective philosophical projects. Rawls's thesis of the priority of the right is tied to his peculiar non-metaphysical conception of the political. He aims to sketch out a free-standing conception of the political that supports his conception of justice as fairness while immunizing it from needless controversy. Habermas's project is broad by comparison. He is interested in all aspects of social order, including its moral, ethical, pragmatic, political, and legal dimensions. Although he thinks that moral considerations must not appeal to controversial cultural values, he denies that the political can be free-standing in the way Rawls thinks it must. On the contrary, the political comprises a whole variety of different mechanisms of resolving conflict that draw freely on the three different kinds of practical discourse.

The tenability of Habermas's distinction between morality and ethics

Habermas asserts that, although the historical distinction between morality and ethics is vague and messy, his conceptual distinction between the two is razor-sharp. He insists that valid norms are fundamentally different from values. The point of a moral discourse in conformity with (U) is to eliminate all values as non-universalizable. Only thus can it function as a rule of argument that makes agreement possible. Habermas wants to remove any lingering suspicion that (U) is just an ethnocentric prejudice resting on a contingent body of values. He argues that the moral principle is rooted in communication and discourse, part of the very fabric of modern societies. Validity claims to rightness and truth govern the coordination of actions and provide the basis for social order. Were he to smudge the distinction between morality and ethics, between moral norms and values, from either direction, then values, which he concedes are a source of intractable conflict, would infiltrate the moral domain and put his whole pragmatic conception of morality in jeopardy.

The trouble is that Habermas's distinction is not as watertight it needs to be. Thomas McCarthy points out that in his haste to reject naturalism (the view that all values can be reduced to empirical facts about human needs and interests), Habermas argues that needs and interests are always already shaped and interpreted in the light of cultural values. Yet he also claims that moral norms embody interests, albeit only universalizable ones. So Habermas concedes, after all, that moral norms depend on values, as the basis on which agents and participants in discourse interpret their interests and needs. Thereby he inadvertently lets values in through the back door, along with their potential for causing moral conflict.

Hilary Putnam has an objection that goes a little further in the same direction. He argues that the distinction between norms and values cannot be sharp, because norms presuppose 'thick ethical concepts' or values. The norms 'be good to your friends', and 'don't be cruel to children', presuppose the values like friendship or cruelty, and without them there is no language in which those norms could be identified and described. If McCarthy and Putnam are right, not only are valid norms scarce, they are unavoidably interlaced with controversial cultural values. In that case, agents will need to find different mechanisms of conflict resolution and seek out other routes to social cooperation and social order than moral ones. That entails a major shift of emphasis for the programme of discourse ethics away from morality and ethics and towards politics and law.

Chapter 8
Politics, democracy, and law

Traditional societies, according to Habermas, are held together by a shared ethos. Upbringing and participation in social practices allow people to acquire the identities and motivations appropriate to the roles and duties that society's institutions require in order to function smoothly. Modern societies are complex, differentiated, and multicultural: they have no controlling centre and are not held together by any single overarching tradition, world view, or set of rules. In modern societies, subjects develop general and abstract identities, which means they don't generally think of themselves primarily as somebody's son or daughter, as part of a family or dynasty, or as citizens of a state; they consider themselves and others first and foremost as individual persons and autonomous, rational beings conducting their own lives by general principles and by particular reasons that apply to them. Their abstract identities persist in spite of changes of nationality, of culture, of country of residence, of career, of name, and so forth. Modern subjectivity is also decentred because the constant and unavoidable pressure to participate in discourse (especially moral discourse) requires ideal role taking, the exchange of perspectives with all others, and the development of what Mead called a larger self (see Chapter 6).

In the original programme of discourse ethics Habermas argued that under modern conditions moral discourse is the primary mechanism of social integration. Moral discourse is appropriate to modern culturally diverse societies, since it allows subjects collectively to determine the rules of their coexistence for themselves, and these rules are highly general and maximally inclusive. Some time in the late 1980s, Habermas realized that morality as described in the original programme is too narrow to fulfil the central social function he allots it. With the introduction of the concept of ethical discourse the revised programme of discourse ethics begins to address this difficulty and Habermas's political theory continues in the same direction. It recognizes that moral discourse alone is not sufficient to regulate conflicts and maintain social order in culturally heterogeneous societies. This is not just because there are so few valid moral norms, nor just because norms themselves may be freighted with controversial values, but also because humans are cut from 'crooked timber' to use Kant's metaphor. If things were otherwise, i.e., if modern agents were reliably disposed to act morally all of the time, then morality alone might be sufficient to keep society up and running. This is evidently not the case.

Habermas's programme of democratic and legal theory begins with the recognition that modern social orders are forged not just by moral norms, but also – and to an increasing degree – by political institutions and laws. In this respect *Between Fact and Norms* complements discourse ethics, and at the same time continues and completes the programme of social theory. One might say (no doubt someone already has) that Habermas's philosophy takes a political turn. If so, that is hardly surprising, since his social and moral theory, argue many of his critics, was always really a political theory in disguise. Even if true, that does not mean that Habermas can afford to drop the moral theory in favour of his political and legal theory. Actually, he cannot do that, because, on his view, politics and law cannot function without morality, and so political and legal theory depend on moral theory.

Habermas's conception of politics

The 'two-track' structure of politics

Habermas distinguishes two basic spheres of politics: the informal and the formal. The informal political sphere consists of a network of spontaneous, 'chaotic' and 'anarchic' sources of communication and discourse. Let us call this sphere 'civil society'. Examples of civil society include voluntary organizations, political associations and the media. The identifying marks of civil society are that it is not institutionalized and that it is not designed to take decisions. By contrast, politics in the formal sense concerns institutional arenas of communication and discourse that are specifically designed to take decisions. Prominent examples include parliaments, cabinets, elected assemblies, and political parties. Note that it is a mistake to think that this formal political sphere is identical with the state. For the state is not just a collection of institutional fora for making policy and taking decisions, it is also an administrative system, a bureaucracy that is steered, to use Habermas's term, by the medium of power.

This two-track conception of informal and formal spheres gives the basic framework of Habermas's conception of politics. In civil society, members of the political community participate in discourse, reach understanding, make compromises and form opinions on matters of particular and general concern. Habermas calls it a process of individual opinion- and will-formation. In the formal political sphere, by contrast, the designated representatives of the members of the political community take decisions, pass laws, formulate and implement policies.

On the picture Habermas paints, a political system functions well when its decision-making institutions are porous to the input of civil society, and it has the right channels through which input from below (civil society and public opinion) can influence its output (policies and laws). In practice, democratic states achieve this balance better than non-democratic systems. Healthy democratic institutions will tend to produce policies and laws that are in tune with discursively formed public opinion, and thus rational or justifiable. This is desirable in itself, and it is also functionally desirable, since modern subjects will tend to abide by policies and laws whose rationale they accept. A rational society is likely to be a stable one. So there are good moral and instrumental reasons why modern subjects prefer to live under democratic institutions.

We must take great care when talking of the ability of democratic systems to come up with justifiable decisions. In the political sphere, the notion of what is justifiable is much broader than it is within the individual domains of theoretical, moral, and ethical discourse. Political justifications comprise a variety of considerations in addition to the epistemic and moral criteria (the validity dimensions of truth and rightness) that govern theoretical and moral discourse respectively. For example, ethical and pragmatic considerations come into play alongside commonsense factors such as what can be achieved by fair procedures of compromise and negotiation. Political discourse is like a workshop in which, once the more demanding procedures of moral and ethical discourses have been tried and have failed, a whole range of other experiments can be made in order to achieve solutions that are broadly speaking rational and consensual.

Human rights and popular sovereignty

Habermas, as is his wont, combines two political conceptions that are usually taken to be alternatives: liberal-democracy and civic republicanism. Each conception, he argues, pivots on a single idea: liberal democracy on the idea of human rights, and civic republicanism on the idea of popular sovereignty. (In actual fact, both conceptions are conjunctions of certain aspects of liberalism and of democracy. In the former, liberalism takes precedence over democracy, in the latter liberalism is subordinate to democracy.) Habermas notes that each conception privileges a certain interpretation of autonomy: liberal-democracy privileges individual or private autonomy (that is, individual self-determination), while civic republicanism privileges collective, public, or political autonomy (that is, the self-realization of the political community).

Habermas states that human rights protect the private autonomy of the individual. On the liberal-democratic view individuals have pre-political interests, and a set of rights that protects their freedom to pursue these interests, compatibly with everyone else's similar freedom to pursue theirs. Freedom here is conceived as an opportunity. The value of my freedom lies in the opportunities it affords me, which I may take up or decline as I please, not in my actual exercise of that freedom. Commonly this view goes hand in hand with the idea of a minimal state that leaves each subject free to pursue her own life as she sees fit, whilst intervening only to resolve the conflicts that arise when one person's freedom impinges on another's. Citizenship or participation in the political community is thus not seen as valuable in itself, but only instrumentally valuable as a means of securing these rights and opportunities.

In order to do this fairly the state must remain neutral with regard to the values and conceptions of the good pursued by its members. That said, the idea of human rights is a moral idea that is inevitably biased against any value or world view that is inconsistent with basic rights and liberties for all. For this reason, many communitarian and republican critics of liberal democracy dispute its supposed neutrality. For their part, most liberals deny that the state must or even can remain neutral in respect of the outcomes or consequences of its policies and laws; they claim only that it should remain neutral in respect of the justification of its policies and laws, in order to steer clear of unnecessary controversy. So while it may not be the case that every law or policy will benefit everyone in the same way and to the same degree, it must be the case that no law is justified on the basis of controversial values.

Popular sovereignty is the idea that the political authority of the state resides ultimately in the will of the people. The idea assumes that politics is essentially a matter of collectively realizing public autonomy, rather than of securing the private autonomy of individuals: It is the freedom of 'we the people' that matters, rather than of each individual. Public autonomy is often conceived on the model of a people's assembly, giving rise to the view that citizens are free to the extent that they are self-legislating. More broadly, popular sovereignty can be construed as the idea that the members of a political community are free to the extent that they can regard the laws that govern them as the expression of their own values.

Unlike the liberal notion of private autonomy, the civic republican idea of public autonomy is not an opportunity concept; it is an exercise concept. The true value of free expression, for example, lies not in the opportunities it affords individuals but in its collective actualization. When enough people exercise their freedom of expression a free press/media and more generally a common culture develops, which is to the benefit of all citizens. Membership in the political community is valuable in itself. Hence the state is anything but neutral; it embodies and actively recommends a set of values and ideals to its citizens. Finally, on this view any individual rights that the subjects enjoy derive from and depend on the values and ideals of the political community.

Habermas's two-track conception of politics provides a framework which marries both ideas, modifying each and tuning them to the realities of modern society. It shows that human rights and popular sovereignty are equiprimordial and reciprocal, which means that neither comes first, and that each mutually depends on the other. At the same time it conjoins, and gives equal weight to, the notions of private and public autonomy. Politics, according to Habermas, is the expression of 'the freedom that springs simultaneously from the subjectivity of the individual and the sovereignty of the people' (BFN, 468). Habermas retains the idea of human rights and broadly subscribes to the liberal view that the state should be inclusive and tolerant of different cultures and world views. However, he denies three key liberal assumptions:

1. that rights belong to pre-political individuals;
2. that membership in the political community is valuable merely as a means to safeguard individual freedom;
3. that the state should remain neutral in respect of the justification of its policies or laws, where neutrality implies avoiding appeal to values and ethical considerations.

Habermas argues that these assumptions reflect the inherent bias towards the subject that characterizes the philosophy of consciousness. He maintains, on the contrary, that rights are only acquired through socialization; that membership of the community is not just instrumentally valuable, and that political justifications should embrace ethical considerations.

At the same time, he rejects three key civic republican assumptions:

1. that the state should embody the values of the political community;
2. that participation in the community is the realization of these values;
3. that subjective rights derive from and depend on the ethical self-understanding of the community.

On his view these assumptions no longer apply because modern societies are made up of a plurality of competing traditions and world views. Therefore the question of which values the state is to recommend and make available to its members will itself be a controversial matter. The most that can be expected is that policies, decisions and laws can find some resonance with the ethical self-understanding of each of its various communities.

Habermas endorses a modern version of the idea of popular sovereignty, shorn of the antiquated view that the people form some kind of person writ large. 'Popular sovereignty is not embodied in a collective subject, or a body politic on the model of an assembly of all citizens', it resides in '"subjectless" forms of communication and discourse circulating through forums and legislative bodies' (BFN,

136). In modern societies, the ideal persists in the extent to which formal decision-making bodies are open to the influence of civil society. When formal political institutions are open to the right degree of input from below, their decisions, policies and laws will tend to be rational and to find acceptance. Since democratic states must be appropriately embedded in civil society, civil society has to be protected for the sake of democracy. This is where the system of rights comes in. Habermas argues that 'the system of rights states the conditions under which the forms of communication necessary for the genesis of legitimate law can be legally institutionalised' (BFN, 103). The basic thought is that a system of rights enshrined in law can help nurture the forms of civil society that formal decision-making bodies need to absorb in order to be able to produce rationally acceptable laws.

Politics and the form of law

Nowadays it can appear to be a truism (albeit one of recent provenance) that society should be organized as a state, with a democratic form of government and a system of human rights. On the face of it this is odd because the liberal individualist idea of human rights and the republican idea of popular sovereignty are inherently in tension. One recommends that government should respect my right to live my life my way (compatibly, of course, with everyone else's right to do it their way); the other champions government by the people.

Habermas does not attempt to deny this. He responds that this tension is rooted in the very concept of law, and that law is the medium which in modern societies helps ease the burden of social integration that falls on communication and moral discourse. Recall that on Habermas's story the social function of morality is to resolve conflicts of interests, coordinate actions, and to establish social order. Politics supports and stabilizes morality by cladding it in the form of law. This does not mean that law and morality cannot come apart. They can and do, for example in cases of civil disobedience and conscientious objection. But these are marginal cases. Generally, legal norms and moral norms work side by side to resolve conflicts, coordinate actions, and produce social order on the basis of valid norms. However, they do so in different ways.

The dual structure of law

Suppose one evening you want ride your bicycle to a party on the other side of town, but you find that it has no lights. There is a law against riding in the dark without lights, and there is a reason for that law: riding without lights endangers the rider and other road users. It is also a punishable offence: if the police see you riding without lights they have the power to apprehend and fine you. Legal norms like this demand only compliance. They require to be obeyed, but they do not require to be obeyed for the right reason. In this they are unlike moral norms, which require to be obeyed for the right reasons. The fear of being caught and punished is not a good moral reason for acting. So the law-abiding agent may either walk to the party because she understands that riding her bicycle without lights endangers herself and other road users, or because it is not worth running the risk of being caught and punished. In practice her motivations are beside the point, since in obeying the law she acts on reasons of road safety that apply to her anyway. Moral and legal norms work in parallel.

Habermas holds that laws produced by political institutions that are open to input from civil society will tend to be rational. Members of the legal community will generally comply with such laws because they will be able to see their point, the laws require them to do what they have independent reasons for doing. Sometimes, however, the point will not suffice to induce lawful behaviour. In such cases, the fear of being apprehended and punished may do the job.

A valid legal norm or law, Habermas argues, has both a normative and a factual side: on the one hand it is legitimate, and on the other it is positive. Hence the title of his book *Between Facts and Norms*, which literally translated would be 'Facticity and Validity'. A law is *legitimate* only when it has a point, or when there are appreciable reasons for obeying it (other than that it is the law, and that disobeying it is a punishable offence.) That its legitimacy is a necessary but not a sufficient condition of the validity of a law becomes evident when we consider two further features of valid laws. A law is *positive* when it is laid down or imposed by a recognized authority. Laws have a third feature too: they must be coercible. A legal norm is valid only when all these components are present. A law must have an appreciable point, be made by a recognized authority, and be coercible. The validity of law thus presupposes political power. It presupposes, among other things, a judiciary and a state which has a monopoly of legitimate force and the ability to enforce laws by policing their observance and punishing their transgression.

The legitimacy of law

Although Habermas acknowledges the positivity and coercibility of law, he always puts the accent on its legitimacy. Legitimate laws, laws with a point, elicit voluntary rational compliance from citizens. Note that rational compliance is different to affective allegiance, although both may be freely given. Affective allegiance may be due to non-rational and non-discursive motives, such as particular values, needs and emotions associated with belonging to a cultural group. Rational compliance is due to the 'motivating force' of good, general reasons (in Habermas's parlance, reasons are by their nature general) that apply independently of legal, judicial and penal institutions. Social order arises smoothly without the threat of punishment having to be brought into action. This is vital since in modern mass societies not all lawful behaviour can be coerced, or induced by threat of sanctions. To a large extent lawful behaviour has to arise freely as a response to the perceived legitimacy of the law.

Habermas formulates his notion of legitimacy in the principle of democracy. The democratic principle is held to be a specification of the discourse principle (D). (D) specifies a necessary condition of the validity of action-norms, that is, it holds for both legal and moral norms. The democratic principle states that:

> Only those laws count as legitimate to which all members of the legal community can assent in a discursive process of legislation that has in turn been legally constituted.

(BFN, 110)

This is another version of the basic Habermasian idea that if something is justified, it must be that everyone can assent to it in a properly prosecuted discourse. According to Habermas, the democratic principle arises from the 'interpenetration' of principle (D) and the legal form. The ins and outs of this process of 'interpenetration' are too complicated to go into here, but the upshot is supposed to be that the legal code and the principle of democracy bring one another into being.

More significantly the legal form enriches principle (D) by introducing differences of scope and justification. The democratic principle states that legitimate laws must be amenable to the assent of all members of the legal community, not of everyone affected by the norm, as in (D). The legal community comprises anyone capable of lawful behaviour, whose actions are governed by the law in question. According to (D), amenability to consensus is a mark of the validity of a norm. The mark of a norm's legitimacy according to the democratic principle is far more complicated. Legitimate laws have to be able to win the assent of all members of the legal community. This assent must be the outcome of a legally constituted process of legislation. In other words a norm is legitimate only if all members of the legal community can assent to it, and they can do so because it has been produced by a formal decision-making body which incorporates deliberation and discourse, is open to input from civil society, and conforms with a legally instituted system of rights. Note that the democratic principle only implies that legitimate laws must merit the assent of all members of the legal community; not that they must actually find it, that everyone must actually agree to every law. In England, there will soon be a law against fox hunting regardless of the views of disgruntled fox hunters. The law was passed in the correct way by a recognized decision-making body, which was open to input by civil society, and considered the representations of the fox hunters. Hence it is legitimate. When the law comes into force, the fact fox hunters do not assent to it, and that they dispute the reasons for its existence will not matter. Assuming that it can in addition be properly policed and enforced, the law will be valid. Habermas's theory of law, like his theory of morality, relies heavily on this distinction between what is in principle amenable to assent, and what in practice finds such assent.

Modernity, law, and morality

Although the legitimacy component of law – its point – is a composite of moral, ethical and pragmatic considerations, morality is the key ingredient. Legitimate law, Habermas argues, 'has a relation to morality inscribed within it.' (BFN, 106) Just what this relation is, is hard to spell out. In German there is an etymological relation. Generally, the English term 'law' is used to translate the German word 'Recht' (as in *Rechtswissenschaft* – jurisprudence); however the same word can also mean 'justice' or 'right'. Presumably, though, Habermas has in mind a conceptual relation between law and morality, not an etymological one. He claims, for example, that legitimate laws must be 'in tune' with moral norms and ethical values (BFN, 99).

Besides being consistent with moral demands, legitimate laws, like moral norms, have an in-built orientation to the common good; that a law is perceptibly in the common good is part of its point. In his earlier work, Habermas tended to assume that legitimate laws are analogous with moral norms, since valid norms are 'equally good for all' and so are also in the common good. The revised programme blocks that assumption. It implies that the common good can mean different things in different contexts. The difference is that moral norms are good for everyone *in the same way* (because

117

they contain universalizable interests), while legal norms are at best good *in some way* for all members of the legal community. The umbrella concept of the common good of the legal community is no longer equivalent with the concept of moral rightness.

Habermas's overall argument seems to be that legitimate law provides a parallel path along which agents can be socialized into post-conventional morality. This is partly because legitimate law is consistent with morality, but also because legitimate law presents agents with the opportunity of seeing and serving the legal common good. Actions which conform to legal norms, and are done because these norms are demonstrably in the common good, are analogous with post-conventional moral actions. Furthermore, citizens of Western democracies can justifiably regard their laws as self-chosen, because their decision-making institutions are open to discourse and input from civil society. To this extent obeying legitimate laws is an orientation according to self-chosen principles, again like post-conventional morality. Hence in highly complex modern societies, which have lost the nexus of a shared ethos, law props up the fragile sphere of morality, and provides legal channels along which 'moral content can spread through a society' even as far as the systems of money and power (BFN, 118).

Objections to Habermas's democratic and legal theory

For all its richness and ingenuity, Habermas's *Between Facts and Norms* faces some serious objections. First, he argues that democratic states must seek the right balance between the input from civil society and the output of formal decision-making bodies, but he does not say what right balance is. Should input from below directly determine the legislative process? Is it better that members of parliament cast their votes on the basis of the actual preferences of their constituents or that they use their own judgement in parliament? After all Habermas recognizes that civil society is anarchic, spontaneous, unconstrained and inherently unstable. Too much input from below would introduce elements of anarchy, spontaneity, and instability into the democratic system, the very problem that beset ancient forms of direct democracy.

Second, Habermas does not make clear to what extent he is recommending a normative ideal of deliberative or discursive democracy and to what extent he is offering an empirical theory. He maintains of course that his theory is both a normative ideal and a description of democracy. That is understandable, since, after all, the very term 'democracy' has normative and descriptive content that is almost impossible to separate. Yet while Habermas is keen to play up the empirical credentials of his theory (for example BFN, 373), he seems less concerned to square it with the relevant empirical data, than to make it backwards-compatible with his other theoretical programmes.

Third, given Habermas's penchant for architectonic, it is surprising that his social theory presents a problem for the political theory. *Between Facts and Norms* identifies two dimensions to political power: communicative and administrative power. Communicative power resides in civil society and in the fora for deliberation and discourse built into decision-making bodies. Administrative power resides in the state and government bureaucracy. Habermas's main thesis is that healthy (democratic) political institutions do and should successfully translate communicative power into administrative power. However, according to Habermas's social theory, the state administration is part of the system steered by instrumental criteria of efficiency, whilst civil society is part of the lifeworld. Institutional arenas of discourse and deliberation are political extrusions of the lifeworld. Now, if the distinction between communicative and instrumental rationality, lifeworld and system, is as strict as Habermas's social theory maintains, and if the integrity of the lifeworld is destroyed by the incursion of the system, how can the desired translation of communicative into administrative power be attained? Why does the civilizing influence of moral and ethical discourse not get blotted out by the iron workings of the administration?

Democracy and critical social theory

As well as answering the guiding question of his sociological project, Habermas's democratic and legal theory can be seen as continuing the project of critical social theory. It does this primarily by diagnosing the strengths and weaknesses of Western democratic states and the dangers facing them. There are two principal dangers. First, if legally enshrined human rights are unable to protect civil society from erosion by markets and administrative bodies, the sources of communication and discourse on which political institutions depend will dry up. If that happens, political decisions will be more prone to ideological distortion and bias towards powerful interest groups. When certain groups are denied input into the legislative process, the laws they live under are likely to appear indifferent or hostile to them, their feelings of marginalization, alienation, and cynicism will grow, and they may gradually begin to pose a threat to social order.

Second, the current style of government in Britain and the U.S. is to delegate decisions to bureaucratic elites 'informed' by experts and interest groups. Parliament and cabinet are used to rubber-stamp policies, rather than as arenas to discuss and deliberate them. Eventually media-savvy officials or 'spin doctors' are used to sell these policies to the public. Manufacturing popular consent is the last step in a chain of otherwise bureaucratic decisions. The tendency is not to promote open and transparent decision-making institutions, but to slough off procedures of communication and discourse from the political process altogether for the sake of expediency, moral 'clarity' or some other supposed benefit. The recent decision by the British government to support U.S. military intervention in Iraq by sending troops there is a case in point. In Britain there were massive and unprecedented popular protests against the policy. The parliamentary vote appeared simply to dot the 'i' on a decision that had already been taken by Tony Blair and his advisors. The second threat is that the civilizing influence of civil society on law- and policy-making bodies diminishes, and that the role of citizens is reduced entirely to that of passive consumers.

In spite of this sober assessment of the dangers facing Western liberal-democracies Habermas retains a flickering optimism in the capacity of democratic institutions to cope with the problems facing modern societies. With all their inherent tensions, liberal-democracies still retain a close link with the ideal of freedom as self-determination. Politics, Habermas states, is the expression of human freedom, understood not as an already established fact, but as an ongoing task imposed by the recognition that, 'No-one is free, until we all are free' (RR, 161).

Chapter 9
Germany, Europe, and post-national citizenship

The previous chapters have shown something of the depth of Habermas's commitment to, and belief in, the beneficial socializing effects of morality, democracy, and individual human rights. Habermas's lifelong antipathy to nationalism in all its forms arises from a clear-sighted and nuanced appreciation of the social pre-conditions of human wrongs, which is rooted in his own experiences. That said, as he would be the first to remind us, we should not confuse the origins of beliefs and convictions with their validity.

Nationhood and nationalism
The idea of the nation state

To understand Habermas's worries about nationalism, we have briefly to examine his conception of the nation. Habermas tells a story in which the European nation comes about as a response to a constellation of social problems that arose at the end of the 18th century. Early modern forms of community had been anchored in locality, structured by rural traditions and a seemingly natural feudal hierarchy, and bound by a shared religious tradition comprising a homogeneous set of cultural values. With the onset of modernity, from the end of the 18th century onwards, a variety of factors – urbanization, the mobility of populations, circulation of goods, and the waning of religion – deprived society of these anchor points. At the same time as the bases of early modern society were disintegrating, a largely urban, mass society of strangers was taking shape.

According to Habermas, the nation emerges as a new, more abstract and more successful basis of social integration. The idea of the nation was more or less concocted from the invented traditions and the fictional history of a single community with a common ancestry, language, and culture. Once the idea caught the public imagination, national consciousness proved very good at creating affective bonds of solidarity between citizens who were also strangers to one another. At the same time, the gradual emergence of democratic participation in the decision-making structures provided a set of legal relations of solidarity between citizens. The ideas of the nation and national consciousness began to work hand in hand with the political structures of the state to imbue its citizens with a sense of belonging to a single political community, and with a sense of their collective cultural and political identity.

While he acknowledges the social achievements of the nation state, Habermas is aware that the idea is also dangerous. The idea of an ethnic nation is inherently exclusionary. Those who belong are always demarcated by language or ancestry from those who do not. Once the idea becomes entrenched in the public mood, it can lead to the creation and oppression of internal minorities. Secondly, relations of nationhood are relations of *affective*, or *emotional* identification with the community that is 'independent of and prior to the political opinion and will formation of citizens themselves' (TIO, 115). These ties are pre-discursive. They are not open to reason. Yet they are easily manipulated by political elites. For example, the surges of national sentiment that accompany foreign military campaigns can quell domestic political unrest, a known effect that governments repeatedly exploit to this day.

While these dangers are built in to the notion of a *community of folk* or *Volksgemeinschaft*, they are not inherent in the ideal of a lawful community of free and equal citizens or *Rechtsgemeinschaft*. Being a citizen or a member of a legal community is a bit like being a student at a university. It is just a place that more or less any Tom, Dick, or Harriet can occupy. Membership is in principle open and it is a political question what the criteria of membership should be. But membership of a national people is a pre-political fact of heredity. Hence, argues Habermas, the concept of the nation state contains a tension between its two halves, 'between the universalism of an egalitarian legal community and the particularism of a community united by historical destiny' (TIO, 115). The challenge to the modern nation state is to live up to its better half.

Nationalism

Nationalism tends to arise when the nation is already under threat. At the beginning of the third millennium, Habermas observes, the nation state is threatened from without by globalization and world-economic pressures, and threatened from within by multiculturalism.

In broad strokes, globalization has led to a situation in which the causes of pressing social and political problems, for example economic migration, poverty, mass unemployment, and the threat of ecological disaster, lie beyond the reach of national politics. Hence so do their possible solutions. Global political problems require transnational political solutions. The problems are exacerbated because the capacities of individual states to act have diminished.

Simultaneously, nations are threatened from within by the emergence of multiculturalism. Immigration and the increasing mobility of people have helped dispel the national myth of a single culturally homogeneous community. Marginalized groups and minorities fight for equal recognition, and challenge the assumptions and certainties of the majority culture.

In this context, nationalism represents a compelling but highly dangerous response. It aims to renew social solidarity and to instil a sense of belonging by reviving national consciousness. Nationalism, in Habermas's view, is not a way of harnessing the resources immanent to the process of modernization – moral discourse and legitimate law – but a futile attempt to reverse the process. It is also, in his estimation, regressive. Recall that, according to Kohlberg, normal children develop upwards through the six stages; they do not travel back down the scale. That would be the case only if they could unlearn. Think how unusual and abnormal it would be for someone to 'unlearn' how to swim or to speak a language. Similarly, contemporary forms of nationalism signal a retreat from post-conventional to conventional forms of association. Nationalism is a kind of social deviancy.

One has to be careful here. Societies only 'learn' in an attenuated sense. So nationalism is *regressive* or *deviant* only in an equally attenuated sense. Habermas does not suggest that the desire to belong to a cultural group is in itself regressive. On the contrary, he recognizes that under conditions of pluralism citizens must situate themselves within traditions and identify with their culture, albeit with the appropriate critical reflection. The regressive aspects of nationalism are the misfired attempts:

1. to replace modern forms of social integration – communication, discourse, and legitimate law – with affective ties of kinship;
2. to find a pre-political, natural criterion of membership in the political community;
3. to remove the influence of discourse and communication from the political process.

Habermas's animus against nationalism may sound overdramatic. Consider, though, that he is all too aware, not just from his childhood experience but from more recent political events in the former Yugoslavia and elsewhere, of the dangers that nationalism poses. The fire of nationalism is easier to ignite than to extinguish, and once reignited, it can lead to the oppression of internal minority groups, to racism, and ultimately to ethnic cleansing and genocide.

Constitutional patriotism

Habermas argues that the only form of identification with one's own traditions that is appropriate under modern conditions is that of constitutional patriotism. He first used this term during a vitriolic public debate in the mid-1980s that came to be known as the 'historian controversy'. Oversimplifying greatly, certain historians with contacts at the heart of Helmut Kohl's government had produced reinterpretations of modern German history that relativized the crimes of the Nazi period, downplayed the significance of the Final Solution, and placed greater emphasis on the heroism of German soldiers who held the Eastern Front in order to allow German civilians to flee from the Red Army.

According to Habermas, the dispute was not about the historical thesis, but about the misuse of academic history for political ends. These strategically revised histories were not merely making validity claims to truth, they also were part of a self-conscious, politically organized attempt to 'normalize' German history, to get rid of the 'past that refused to go away'. Among the medium-term aims of this campaign was the wish to help create a German national identity, and thereby to bolster Helmut Kohl's popularity at home. The envisaged end game may have been to prepare the political ground for West Germany to cease paying reparations to Israel, and to begin playing a geo-political role that would reflect its economic power. Hitherto it had been assumed that the path to 'normalization' was barred by an insuperable obstacle: Auschwitz. German national consciousness had been indelibly tainted by the moral catastrophe of 1933–45.

Against this backdrop, Habermas argued that the tactic of manufacturing a past Germany could feel proud of was futile and regressive. The only form of patriotism that was politically and morally appropriate was one that was anchored in the universal principles of the constitutional state.

> For us in the Federal Republic constitutional patriotism means, among other things, pride in the fact that we have succeeded in permanently overcoming fascism, establishing a just political order, and in anchoring it in a fairly liberal political culture.

> (NR, 152)

It is important to remember that the Basic Law of the Federal Republic of Germany had been imposed upon it by an alien conquering power. It was not the expression of an authentic German tradition of democratic politics. At the time of its creation, the Basic Law was a provisional democratic constitution in search of democratic citizens. Yet by the mid-1980s West Germany had become one of the most thriving democracies in Europe. That, Habermas thought, was an achievement to be proud of. By a good measure of historical luck, a lot of hard work, and a successful policy of re-education, the citizens of the Federal Republic had developed a political culture and a political identity based on a commitment to democratic procedures and principles.

> The political culture of a country crystallizes around its constitution. Each national culture develops a distinctive interpretation of those constitutional principles . . . such as popular sovereignty and human rights – in the light of its own national history. A 'constitutional patriotism' based on these interpretations can take the place originally occupied by nationalism.

> (TIO, 118)

On this picture, German political identity is paradoxical. It was largely because their difficult past refused to go away that West Germans had to forge a political identity around the 'universalistic content of the democratic constitutional state' and to forswear more historically naive, less critically reflective forms of patriotism. By being true to their own (but deeply ambivalent) German tradition, they were obliged to identify less, not more closely with it.

When Habermas first began to defend the notion of constitutional patriotism in the 1980s, he had not yet fully developed his ideas on the political significance of ethical discourse. He tended to align democratic principles with moral ones. Just as the post-conventional moral subject is committed not to substantive values of the community, but to the procedure by which valid norms are established, so the constitutional patriot identifies with democratic procedures rather than with specific outcomes. Both develop decentred and abstract identities to the extent that morality and democracy involve the recognition of the equal worth of others. Moreover, he argued, citizens identify directly with universal democratic and moral principles.

In his later work, Habermas alters his view. He argues that for a democratic constitution to take root it must be supported by a political culture that satisfies various conditions. First, it must be consistent with post-conventional morality. Second, it must resonate with the ethical understanding of all cultural groups in the political community. The political culture cannot afford to be seen as an expression of the substantive and particular values of the majority culture. Finally, the political culture needs to be supported by social and welfare rights, in order that citizens can experience 'the fair value of their rights', that is that they can feel the benefit of their participation in the common political culture.

German unification

The 9th of November 1989 represented a turning point in the lives of all Germans: the Berlin Wall came down and the German Democratic Republic collapsed. At the time, Habermas voiced some serious critical reservations about the way in which unification was being carried out, its timing, and the political rationale behind these.

13. East German citizens sit astride the Berlin Wall

His criticisms were initially directed at the procedural question
of whether unification should be accomplished on the basis of
Article 23 of the Basic Law or Article 146. Article 146 makes
clear that the Basic Law is a provisional, not yet a fully fledged,
constitution. It states: 'this Basic Law loses its validity on the
day that a new constitution takes effect, concluded by the German
people in a free decision'. Article 23 makes the Basic Law
valid for other parts of Germany. It provides a mechanism for
granting new states entry into the federation. It was written
principally with the region of the Saarland, on the border with
France, in mind.

Kohl and his advisors preferred to base unification on Article 23,
since it did not require any change in the West German Basic Law.
Habermas vehemently opposed this. In his eyes, unification on the
basis of Article 23 was a purely administrative manoeuvre by which
East Germany could be effectively annexed by West Germany.
Worse still, this strategy was chosen so that the whole process could
be managed in the particular domestic and foreign policy interests
of Chancellor Kohl's Christian Democrats. Use of Article 23 meant

that the process could be completed relatively swiftly, in order to boost Kohl's domestic popularity in time for the coming elections.

As a consequence, East and West Germans were deprived of the opportunity for an ethical-political discourse about the kinds of political structures under which they would prefer to live. Habermas was one of several intellectuals at the time who argued for a slower pace of reform and a more inclusive process. Unification should have been 'the public act of a carefully considered democratic decision taken in both parts of Germany' (YAGI, 96). East Germans would have been able to have some input into the process, instead of having everything done for them by bureaucrats in the West, and West Germans would have been able to vote on their own constitution. As it was, Habermas complained of the 'normative deficit' of unification, because the union lacked sufficient political, ethical, and moral justification – the kind of input from below that he takes to be a necessary condition of democratic legitimacy.

On similar grounds, Habermas objected to the administrative 'liquidation' of all the old institutions that harboured the remnants of East German civil society – universities, colleges, museums, theatres, and so on. He warned that civil society, by which he meant informal networks of public communication and discourse, is a fragile and valuable political resource that is much easier to destroy than to rebuild. Habermas argued that unification was not just an administrative and economic fact, but also a political task, and hence that a political culture that could find some resonance with the self-understanding of the East Germans had to be allowed to grow.

Finally, Habermas suspected that the incumbent Christian Democratic government might be tempted to legitimate their policies by encouraging pan-German nationalist sentiment. Initially, they had been content to appeal to economic nationalism. On the one hand, they reminded the citizens of the Federal

Republic how well they had done up to now, and made the unkeepable promise that they (the West Germans) would not have to underwrite the costs of unification through higher taxes. On the other, they offered East German citizens a vision of similar economic prosperity. Habermas's thought, encapsulated in the slogan 'a unified nation of angry DM-Burghers?', was that when the realization eventually dawned that the economic rebuilding of the East would be slow, painful, and costly, and not funded entirely through economic growth, German citizens both East and West would feel betrayed. The easy way out of this problem would be to fan the flames of German nationalism, with all its attendant dangers. The outbreaks of racist violence against foreign guest-workers at Rostock and Hoyerswerda in East Germany shortly after the initial euphoria of unification signalled these dangers all too clearly.

Habermas warned conservatives not to jeopardize the hard-won but fragile political culture of West Germany – a non-nationalist self-understanding, post-national collective identity, and constitutional patriotism. Instead of the bland appeal to economic nationalism, Habermas called for a process of 'reunification which gives priority to the freely exercised right of the citizens to determine their own future by direct vote, within the framework of a non-occupied public sphere . . . ' (YAGI, 96). A slower-paced process, based on Article 146, would give time and space for the required moral, ethical, and political discourses that could allow relations of mutual solidarity to grow between the citizens of the former East and West German states. In turn, this would encourage German citizens to evaluate the question from a wider perspective than that of their individual self-interest.

European integration

Habermas's views on the question of European integration are in line with his observations on the obsolescence of the nation and his political and moral animus against nationalism. He adduces several different sets of considerations in favour of economic and political union of European states.

Germany and the European question

First, there are a set of broadly historical and moral reasons, which fall under the Habermasian theme of 'learning from catastrophe'. One only has to look back to recent 20th-century history, the catastrophes of two world wars, to appreciate the dangers of a Europe of sovereign nation states in economic and political competition with each other. Europeans, he argues, 'must abandon the mind-sets on which nationalistic and exclusionary mechanisms feed' (TIO, 152). Political union would provide a framework within which a post-national social integration could develop on the basis of 'the communicative network of a European-wide political public sphere embedded in a shared political culture'.

I suggest that even this project can be understood as a very concrete political way of answering Adorno's new categorical imperative: to prevent the reoccurrence of Auschwitz or anything similar. Given the peculiarities of its recent past, European integration is all the more vital for Germany. Habermas vociferously opposed what he considered to be the ugly and dangerous suggestions in some conservative circles for Germany to halt its slide towards the European Union, to keep the Deutschmark, and to forge political and economic links with the central European states now liberated from Soviet communism.

Another set of arguments in favour of European integration concerns the effects of a globalized economy on the individual nation state. Generally speaking, the governments of developed and technically advanced industrial states know that economic growth comes at a certain social and political cost: increases in unemployment, poverty, and income disparities. Left uncontained these effects would be potential causes of social disintegration and internal political destabilization. To an extent, however, welfare states have been able to contain these negative effects by means of welfare systems, labour market regulation, and redistributive policies, among other measures.

The globalization of the economy and financial markets has altered the delicate balance between economic growth and social welfare. Globalization has had the effect of tying the hands of the governments of individual nation states. Large corporations can easily evade employment regulations by relocating to countries where markets are unregulated and labour is cheap. The threat of 'capital flight' forces governments of whatever stripe to keep taxes (particularly business and corporation taxes) low. Raising revenues becomes a problem for governments. There is a limit to how much money can be made through efficiency savings. In short, it becomes difficult for governments of individual states to fund and implement policies that contain the undesirable social and political side effects of capitalist economic growth.

In Habermas's eyes, there are two possible responses to these problems. The neo-liberal alternative is simply to adapt to global economic pressures: drive down costs, keep labour markets 'flexible' (that is, unregulated), and put the onus on individuals to insure themselves against the risks of unemployment, ill health, and so on. The bitter pill is that the economic winners of a competition to deregulate will be the social and political losers.

The other alternative is that politics must globalize too, in order to rein in the economy. In concrete terms, this means creating supra-national political institutions with the authority, power, and means to implement their resolutions. At first blush, this may appear hopelessly Utopian. Habermas responds that, once one has accepted the impending obsolescence of the nation state as a political entity, there is only one viable alternative, and the expansion of politics beyond the nation state is already under way.

The European Union is, in relative terms, an ambitious example of what can be done.

Of course the European Union will only provide an effective counterweight to global economic pressures if it can find functional equivalents at the supra-national level for the containing functions of the welfare state. European Union policies have been able, through the introduction of subsidies and other modest redistributive policies, to eliminate some of the harmful effects of regional competition between member states. Further, the European Court of Justice has taken hundreds of decisions that bear directly on questions of social justice and (to the consternation of its neo-liberal and Tory critics in Britain) that indirectly affect the common internal market. Habermas does not underestimate the difficulties that beset the project of European economic and political integration. The European Union still has to juggle the conflicting aims of employment, competitiveness, and economic growth, and negotiate settlements between demands of rich member states who are net-contributors and poor member states who are net-beneficiaries. For Habermas, it has yet to be established whether the European Union can formulate and implement policies capable of correcting markets, and bringing them into line with ideals of social justice.

Habermas concedes that, from a global perspective, European politics is really just an extension, not a transformation, of the politics of national self-interest. Regional competition between nation states and its attendant problems occurs again at the transnational level. Europe vies with its competitors, the United States, the Pacific Rim, and the emerging economies of China and India. Hence there are reasons to suspect that it will not be able to find lasting and comprehensive solutions to global political and social problems, and that at most it will provide temporary or partial solutions. Habermas grasps the logic of his own argument. If lasting and effective political solutions to global problems are to be found, they must be sought ultimately at the level of a cosmopolitan world politics. If supra-national political institutions are to rein in global markets, they have to be properly inclusive. The ultimate aim is for the creation of a world internal market, and a political entity with the authority and power to regulate it. The ultimate aim is for the creation of a political united nations with the power not just to make resolutions, but to implement them.

The legitimation deficit

The trouble is that European political institutions suffer from what is known as a 'democratic deficit'. Eurosceptics argue that a political union cannot succeed, because there is no European 'people' for the institutions to represent. There is nothing substantial – no shared history, no common language, tradition, or ethnicity – to generate the bonds of solidarity between citizens on which democracy depends.

Habermas admits that there is no European 'people', but he denies that the existence of a European people or nation with a common history and descent is a necessary basis for social integration. It is true, he argues, that the thick notion of citizenship based on a common national consciousness cannot be stretched further than the boundaries of a single nation. It cannot even be stretched that far. For reasons outlined above, the antiquated conception of the nation is no longer appropriate to modern multicultural societies. Eurosceptics who dismiss the project of European integration and prefer to shelter in their little hut will soon find that the floor is rotten and the roof has fallen in. Modern multicultural societies are not communities of a single people or folk; they are lawful communities of citizens. This thin conception of democratic citizenship as an abstract, legally mediated relation between strangers can be stretched to include inhabitants of foreign countries. Habermas does not attempt to deny that there is a democratic deficit in the European Union.

> As new organisations emerge even further removed from the political base, such as the Brussels bureaucracy, the gap between

self-programming administrations and systemic networks, on the one hand, and democratic processes, on the other, grow constantly.

(TIO, 151)

But he argues that there is no reason in principle why this gap should not be filled. Modern democratic societies are integrated through spheres of informal public communication, and institutional arenas for discourse and decision-making.

One pressing, but not necessarily insoluble, problem is how to encourage the development of a Europe-wide network of discourse and communication, of a European civil-society and political culture. He argues that,

> there can be no European federal state worthy of the title of a European democracy unless a European-wide, integrated public sphere develops in the ambit of a common political culture: a civil society encompassing interest associations, nongovernmental organizations, citizens' movements, etc., and naturally a party system appropriate to a European arena.
>
> (TIO 160)

Educational exchange programmes, increased economic cooperation, easier travel between member states, and the development of a European party system will all contribute to this end.

Another practical and institutional problem is to think of ways of connecting the European bureaucracy and parliament to this developing political culture. That might be hard, but not impossible. However, to cling to the belief in the political efficacy of the nation state, in flagrant disregard of the evidence, is futile; and to allow free rein to global economic markets is socially and politically unconscionable.

According to Habermas, European integration may not be the

ultimate end point of post-national politics, but it is at least an auspicious beginning. The European Union is an ongoing experiment in post-national democratic politics. As Habermas elegantly puts it, in a dialogue with Michael Haller entitled 'Europe's Second Chance':

> If there is any small remnant of utopia that I've preserved, then it is surely the idea that democracy – and its public struggle for its best form – is capable of hacking through the Gordian knots of otherwise insoluble problems. I'm not saying we're going to succeed in this; we don't even know whether success is possible. But because we don't know we still have to try.

(TPF, 97)

Although we don't know whether the European Union will succeed in providing partial solutions to post-national problems, or perhaps even be a platform for an eventual cosmopolitan world order, we don't know that it will fail either. The experiment must be continued, Habermas suggests, above all because we do know that the alternative is worse: to say farewell to the idea of democratic politics as the attempt of free and equal citizens collectively to shape their social world.

Appendix: Summary of Habermas's five major research programmes

1. The pragmatic meaning programme

Basic questions: How does one understand the meaning of utterances? What is the pragmatic function of speech? How does speech coordinate the actions of social agents? What is the relation between validity and meaning? What kinds of validity claim are there?

Basic answers: There are two kinds of meaning – performative (pragmatic) and propositional. The pragmatic function of speech is to elicit rational consensus. Speech coordinates actions through validity claims. The validity of an utterance determines how its meaning is understood. There are three kinds of validity claim – to truth, to rightness, and to truthfulness.

2. The theory of communicative rationality

Basic questions: What are the fundamental types of action? What is the difference between them? Which type is prior or more fundamental? In virtue of what?

Basic answers: There are two types of action: communicative action on the one hand, instrumental and strategic action on the other. The difference is that communicative actions aim at securing understanding and consensus, while instrumental and strategic actions aim at practical success. Communicative action is the more fundamental because it is self-standing; instrumental and strategic action are not.

3. The programme of social theory

i) The sociological project

Basic questions: How is social order possible? What holds modern societies together? How are actions of millions of social agents coordinated?

Basic answers: Social order rests on meaning and validity, and on the integrity of a lifeworld maintained by communication and discourse. It also rests to a degree on the integrating force of instrumental and strategic actions within systems such as markets and administrations. Shared meanings, understandings, and reasons hold society together, along with organized systems of instrumental rationality.

ii) The social ontology

Basic questions: What are modern societies like? Of what are they made up?

Basic answers: Modern societies are made up out of two kinds of social being – the lifeworld and the system. The lifeworld is the home of communication and discourse. The system is the home of instrumental and strategic actions.

iii) Critical social theory

Basic questions: What is the underlying cause of the pathologies of modern social life? Why do people by and large accept and maintain social systems that are not in their interests? What are the most pressing current threats to the maintenance of the lifeworld? What can be done about them?

Basic answers: Systems – markets and administrations – expand and colonize the lifeworld, the home of communicative action and discourse, on which they themselves depend. People are forced into patterns of instrumental and strategic action and become divorced from their ultimate goals; consequently they experience loss of meaning and autonomy. The lifeworld needs to be kept intact, and the ill-effects of the systems' intrusion into non-system domains mitigated.

4. The programme of discourse ethics

i) The discourse theory of morality

Basic questions: How is moral order possible? What makes an action morally right or wrong? How do we know, and how do we learn, what is right/wrong?

Basic answers: Moral order rests on the existence of demonstrably valid norms and the fact that most agents are disposed to adhere to them. What makes an action right/wrong is that it is permitted/ prohibited by a valid moral norm. What makes a norm valid is that it demonstrably embodies a universal interest. We find out whether this is the case by testing candidate norms for their capacity to elicit rational agreement in moral discourse.

ii) The discourse theory of ethics

Basic questions: What is distinctive about ethical as opposed to moral questions? What is the social and political significance of ethical questions?

Basic answers: Ethical discourse concerns questions of individual happiness and the good of communities. Ethical discourse involves critical appropriation of traditions and the interpretation of values.

5. The programme of political theory

i) The discourse theory of politics

Basic questions: How is a well-ordered political system possible? What makes laws, policies, and political decisions legitimate?

Basic answers: A well-ordered political system is one in which the right balance between private and public autonomy is achieved and in which political order is stabilized to a large degree by rational decisions produced by institutions that are sensitive to the informal public spheres of civil society. Laws are legitimate only if they are in tune with the opinions, values, and norms generated discursively in civil society.

ii) The discourse theory of law

Basic questions: What is a valid law? What is the role of valid legal norms?

Basic answers: A valid law is a law that is positive, enforceable, and legitimate. Legitimate laws must be consistent with moral, ethical, and pragmatic considerations and serve the good of the legal community. Valid legal norms authorize and implement political power. They support moral norms, help to harmonize individual action and to establish social order.

Further Reading

All the books and articles listed here are in English. Dates in square brackets indicate the year of original publication in German.

A selection of Habermas's early writings

Structural Transformation of the Public Sphere: An Inquiry into a Category of Bourgeois Society, tr. T. Burger and F. Lawrence (Cambridge, Mass.: MIT Press, 1989 [1962]).

Theory and Practice, tr. John Viertel (Cambridge: Polity Press, 1988 [1963]). An abridged collection of critical thematic and historical essays on social theory which includes the seminal essay on 'labour and interaction', the key to Habermas's understanding of Hegel, and to his critique of Marx and Marxism.

On the Logic of the Social Sciences, tr. Shierry Weber Nicholsen and Jerry A. Stark (Cambridge, Mass.: MIT Press, 1988 [1967]).

Knowledge and Human Interests, tr. Jeremy J. Shapiro (Boston: Beacon Press, 1971 [1968]). In this book, Habermas examines the role of reflection in critical social theory. It contains a critique of the idealist philosophies of Kant and Fichte, Habermas's engagement with pragmatism and hermeneutic philosophy, and an interesting appropriation of Freud.

Towards a Rational Society, tr. Jeremy J. Shapiro (Boston: Beacon Press, 1987 [1969]). Contains three essays on the student protests and three essays on the role of technology and science.

Legitimation Crisis, tr. Thomas McCarthy (London: Heinemann, 1976 [1973]). An interesting early study of crisis and legitimacy in capitalist societies in which Habermas puts the distinction between lifeworld and system to work.

Communication and the Evolution of Society, tr. Thomas McCarthy (London: Heinemann Educational Books, 1979 [1976]). This is an important study in Habermas's reconstruction of historical materialism, in which he looks at the role of moral development of individuals and social structures.

A selection of Habermas's mature theoretical writings

Pragmatic theory of meaning and theory of communicative rationality

The Theory of Communicative Action, tr. Thomas McCarthy, vol. 1 (Cambridge: Polity Press, 1984 [1981]). The pragmatic theory of meaning and the theory of communicative rationality are set out in Part III, 'Intermediate Reflections'. Part IV contains criticisms of Weber, Lukacs, and Adorno.

Post-Metaphysical Thinking: Philosophical Essays, tr. William Mark Hohengarten (Cambridge: Polity Press, 1992 [1988]). A collection of essays on Habermas's conception of philosophy, some of which are relevant to programmes 1, 2, and 4.

The following two collections contain mainly articles on programmes 1 and 2. *On the Pragmatics of Social Interaction: Preliminary Studies in the Theory of Communicative Action*, tr. Barbara Fultner (Oxford: Blackwell, 2003 [1984]). *On the Pragmatics of Communication*, ed. Maeve Cooke (Cambridge, Mass.: MIT Press, 2000).

Truth and Justification: Philosophical Essays, tr. B. Fultner
(Cambridge: Polity Press, 2003 [1999]) is a collection of Habermas's
more recent studies on truth and on the pragmatic theory of meaning.
Part III contains a surprising revision to Habermas's theory of truth that
has important ramifications for discourse ethics.

Social theory

The lion's share of Habermas's social theory is contained in *The Theory
of Communicative Action*, vol. 2, tr. Thomas McCarthy (Cambridge:
Polity Press, 1987 [1981]), Part VI, 'Intermediate Reflections', and
Part VIII.

Discourse ethics

Moral Consciousness and Communicative Action, tr. Christian
Lenhardt and Shierry Weber Nicholsen (Cambridge: Polity Press,
1990 [1983]). This is a collection of seminal essays on the programme
of discourse ethics. It should be read alongside the later collection,
Justification and Application, tr. C. Cronin (Cambridge: Polity Press,
1993 [1991]), an important collection of essays, in which Habermas
responds to criticisms and develops the distinction between morality
and ethics.

Political and legal theory

'Law and Morality', tr. Kenneth Baynes, in *The Tanner Lectures on
Human Values*, vol. 8, ed. Sterling M. McMurrin (Salt Lake City:
University of Utah Press, 1988), pp. 217–79. The Tanner Lectures
were held four years before the publication of *Faktizität und Geltung*,
Habermas's major work on political and legal theory. The English
translation of *Faktizität und Geltung* is *Between Facts and Norms*, tr.
William Rehg (Cambridge: Polity Press in association with Blackwell,
1996) and it contains two important earlier essays in addition.
Programme 5 is set out mainly in chapters 3, 4, 7, and 8.

The Inclusion of the Other, tr. C. Cronin and P. De Greiff (Cambridge:
Polity Press, 1998 [1996]). A collection of essays on Habermas's moral

and political theory that contains his critique of Rawls and three studies
on the nation state.

Theory of modernity

The Philosophical Discourse of Modernity: Twelve Lectures, tr. F.
Lawrence (Cambridge: Polity Press, 1987 [1985]). In these lectures,
Habermas engages polemically with French poststructuralist thought,
and develops his critique of Adorno and Horkheimer. See also
Habermas's 1980 essay 'Modernity: An Unfinished Project', tr. Nicholas
Walker, and reprinted in *Habermas and the Unfinished Project of
Modernity: Critical Essays on the Philosophical Discourse of Modernity*,
ed. Seyla Benhabib and Maurizio Passerin d'Entrèves (Cambridge,
Mass.: MIT Press, 1997).

Other work

The Future of Human Nature (Cambridge: Polity Press, 2003 [2001])
brings together some of Habermas's essays on the moral, ethical, and
political implications of bioethics and gene technology.

A selection of Habermas's occasional political writings and interviews

The New Conservatism: Cultural Criticism and the Historian's Debate,
ed. and tr. Shierry Weber Nicholsen (Cambridge, Mass.: MIT Press,
1989).

'What Does Socialism Mean Today?', *New Left Review*, 183:
3–21.

'Yet Again German National Identity – A Nation of Angry DM-
Burghers?' in *When the Wall Came Down: Reactions to German
Unification*, ed. Harold James and Maria Stone (New York: Routledge,
1992).

Autonomy and Solidarity: Interviews with Jürgen Habermas, ed. P.
Dews, revised and enlarged edn. (London: Verso, 1992).

Habermas

The Past as Future: Jürgen Habermas Interviewed by Michael Haller, tr. Max Pensky (Cambridge: Polity Press, 1994).

A Berlin Republic: Writings on Germany, tr. S. Rendall (Lincoln: University of Nebraska Press, 1997).

The Post National Constellation, tr. and ed. Max Pensky (Cambridge: Polity Press, 2001).

Philosophy in a Time of Terror: Dialogues with Jürgen Habermas and Jacques Derrida, ed. Giovanna Borradori (Chicago: University of Chicago Press, 2003).

Time of Transitions, tr. Max Pensky (Cambridge: Polity Press, 2005)

A selection of recent monographs

Pragmatic theory of meaning and theory of communicative rationality

Language and Reason, ed. Maeve Cooke (Cambridge, Mass.: MIT Press, 1994). The first full study in English on Habermas's pragmatic theory of meaning and theory of communicative rationality.

Social theory

Communicative Action and Rational Choice, Joseph Heath (Cambridge, Mass.: MIT Press, 2001). Though not easy reading, this is a detailed and impressive analysis of Habermas's social theory and its philosophical underpinnings. It brings Habermas's philosophy into dialogue with analytic philosophy of language and rational choice theory, and also covers programmes 1, 2, and 4.

Discourse ethics

Insight and Solidarity: The Discourse Ethics of Jürgen Habermas, William Rehg (Berkeley: University of California Press, 1994). A comprehensive critical elucidation and defence of Habermas's programme of discourse ethics.

Making Moral Sense: Beyond Habermas and Gauthier, Logi Gunnarsson (Cambridge: Cambridge University Press, 2000). A critical comparison of Habermas and Gauthier's rationalist justification of moral theory with the substantivist approach attributed to John McDowell.

Impartiality in Context: Grounding Justice in a Pluralist World, Shane O'Neill (Albany: SUNY Press, 1997). An interesting discussion of Habermas's discourse ethics against the backdrop of sectarian conflict in Northern Ireland.

Political and legal theory

The Normative Grounds of Social Criticism: Kant, Rawls and Habermas, Kenneth Baynes (Albany: SUNY Press, 1992). An important study on Habermas's politics providing a comparison of Habermas and Rawls. See also *Reasonable Democracy: Jürgen Habermas and the Politics of Discourse*, ed. Simone Chambers (Ithaca: Cornell University Press, 1996).

Theory of modernity

Between Reason and History: Habermas and the Idea of Progress, David S. Owen (Albany: SUNY Press, 2002).

Other works

Another Country: German Intellectuals, Unification and National Identity, Jan Werner Müller (New Haven: Yale University Press, 2000). Contains a critical analysis of Habermas's views on German unification.

Jürgen Habermas: A Philosophical-Political Profile, Martin Beck Matustík (Lanham: Rowman and Littlefield, 2001). Quirky biography with an emphasis on Habermas's complex and strained relations to the student movement in the 1960s.

Habermas: A Critical Introduction, William Outhwaite (Oxford: Blackwell, 1994).

The Philosophy of Habermas, Andrew Edgar (Teddington: Acumen, 2004).

Collections of essays on Habermas's theoretical work

Habermas: Critical Debates, ed. J. B. Thompson and D. Held (London: Macmillan, 1982). This is not recent, but is still a valuable collection that contains Habermas's replies to his critics. Addresses programmes 1, 2, and 3.

Communicative Action: Essays on Jürgen Habermas's 'The Theory of Communicative Action', ed. Axel Honneth and Hans Joas, tr. Jeremy Gains and Doris L. Jones (Cambridge: Polity Press, 1991). Collects together some critical responses to *The Theory of Communicative Action*. Covers programmes 1, 2, and 3.

The Communicative Ethics Controversy, ed. Seyla Benhabib and F. Dallmayr (Cambridge, Mass.: MIT Press, 1990). A useful collection of material on discourse ethics. Programme 4.

Ideals and Illusions: On Reconstruction and Deconstruction in Contemporary Critical Theory, Thomas McCarthy (Cambridge, Mass.: MIT Press, 1991). A collection of essays by Habermas's most longstanding critic and intellectual fellow traveller. Deals with programmes 3, 4, and 5.

Philosophical Interventions in the Unfinished Project of Enlightenment, ed. Axel Honneth et al., tr. William Rehg (Cambridge, Mass.: MIT Press, 1992) and *Cultural-Political Interventions in the Unfinished Project of Enlightenment*, ed. Axel Honneth et al., tr. Barbara Fultner (Cambridge, Mass.: MIT Press, 1992). These two companion volumes contain critical responses to all aspects of Habermas's philosophy. The list of contributors reads like a 'Who's Who?' of social theory. Examines programmes 2, 3, 4, and 5.

Habermas and the Unfinished Project of Modernity: Critical Essays on the Philosophical Discourse of Modernity, ed. Seyla Benhabib and Maurizio Passerin d'Entrèves (Cambridge, Mass.: MIT Press, 1997).

Habermas and the Public Sphere, ed. C. Calhoun (Cambridge, Mass.: MIT Press, 1992). Critical responses to *Strukturwandel der Öffentlichkeit* subsequent to its English translation. Many of these essays look at Habermas's early book in the light of his mature social theory and the programme of discourse ethics, and so are relevant to programmes 3, 4, and 5.

Feminists Read Habermas: Gendering the Subject of Discourse, ed. Johanna Meehan (London: Routledge, 1995). Feminist responses to Habermas's philosophy.

The Cambridge Companion to Habermas, ed. S. K. White (Cambridge: Cambridge University Press, 1995). An uneven collection of essays that includes valuable contributions by Max Pensky, Ken Baynes, and Simone Chambers (chapters 4, 7, and 8) on Habermas's politics, and on his political and democratic theory respectively. Focuses on programmes 3, 4, and 5.

Habermas: A Critical Reader, ed. P. Dews (Oxford: Blackwell, 1999). A collection of essays that attempt to situate Habermas's theories in the context of the various philosophical traditions in which he works.

Perspectives on Habermas, ed. Lewis Edwin Hahn (Illinois: Open Court, 2000). A large collection of critical and comparative essays addressing programmes 3, 4, and 5.

Habermas, Modernity and Law, ed. Mathieu Deflem (London: Sage, 1996). Looks at programme 5.

Habermas on Law and Democracy: Critical Exchanges, ed. M. Rosenfeld and A. Arato (Berkeley: University of California Press, 1998). Large collection of critical responses to *Between Facts and Norms*. Programme 5.

Discourse and Democracy: Essays on Habermas's Between Facts and Norms, ed. René von Schomberg and Kenneth Baynes (Albany: SUNY Press, 2002). Programme 5.

Habermas and Pragmatism, ed. M. Aboulafia, M. Bookman, and C. Kemp (London: Routledge, 2002). A collection of essays exploring the pragmatic aspects of Habermas's work and his idiosyncratic relation to the tradition of American pragmatism. Contains material relevant to programmes 1, 3, and 5.

Selection of the author's work on Habermas and the Frankfurt School

'Habermas's Discourse Ethics and Hegel's Critique of Kant's Moral Theory', in *Habermas: A Critical Reader*, ed. P. Dews (Oxford: Blackwell, 1999), 29–52.

'What are Universalizable Interests?', *Journal of Political Philosophy*, 8: 4 (2000): 446–72.

'Modernity and Morality in Habermas's Discourse Ethics', *Inquiry*, 3 (2000): 319–40.

'Adorno on the Ethical and the Ineffable', *European Journal of Philosophy*, 10, 1 (2002): 1–25.

Review of Logi Gunnarsson, 'Making Moral Sense: Beyond Habermas and Gauthier', *Ethics*, 112, 4 (2002): 828–31.

'Theory of Ideology and the Ideology of Theory: Habermas contra Adorno', *Historical Materialism*, 11, 2 (2003): 165–87.

'Habermas's Moral Cognitivism and the Frege-Geach Challenge', *European Journal of Philosophy*, (2005 forthcoming).

Index

Habermas

Visit the
VERY SHORT INTRODUCTIONS
Web site

www.oup.co.uk/vsi

➤ **Information** about all published titles

➤ News of **forthcoming books**

➤ **Extracts** from the books, including titles
not yet published

➤ **Reviews** and views

➤ **Links** to other **web sites** and main
OUP web page

➤ Information about **VSIs in translation**

➤ **Contact** the editors

➤ **Order** other **VSIs** on-line

MARX
A Very Short Introduction
Peter Singer

Peter Singer has succeeded in identifying the central vision that unifies Marx's thought. He thus makes it possible, in remarkably few pages, for us to grasp Marx's views as a whole, rather than as an economist or a social scientist. He explains alienation, historical materialism, the economic theory of Capital and Marx's ideas of communism in plain English, and concludes with an assessment of Marx's legacy.

'An admirably balanced portrait of the man and his achievement.'

Philip Toynbee, *Observer*

www.oup.co.uk/isbn/0-19-285405-4

ONLINE CATALOGUE
A Very Short Introduction

Our online catalogue is designed to make it easy to find your
ideal Very Short Introduction. View the entire collection by subject
area, watch author videos, read sample chapters, and download
reading guides.

SOCIAL MEDIA
Very Short Introduction

Join our community

www.oup.com/vsi

- Join us online at the official Very Short Introductions **Facebook** page.
- Access the thoughts and musings of our authors with our online **blog**.
- Sign up for our monthly **e-newsletter** to receive information on all new titles publishing that month.
- Browse the full range of Very Short Introductions online.
- Read **extracts** from the Introductions for free.
- Visit our library of **Reading Guides**. These guides, written by our expert authors will help you to question again, why you think what you think.
- If you are a teacher or lecturer you can order inspection copies quickly and simply via our website.